Simple Real Food

Delicious clean food prepared simply

By Amanda Cushman

Contents

Acknowledgements

I thank my family who started my journey with food over forty years ago. Without my mother Marylin and my aunt Katherine cooking fabulous meals all those years, this career would not have started.

Thanks to my friends who encouraged me with their appreciation and enthusiasm for the meals I prepared. They have always been, and are to this day, my biggest fans.

I especially thank Janice Vanghele for her support and professional advice throughout the process of putting this book together.

My editor and proof-reader Andrea Hoberman has been a big part of the completion of Simple Real Food. She did all the work I couldn't do and was an invaluable part of this book.

I also thank the many students whom I have taught for over fourteen years in New York City and Los Angeles who have pushed me to publish this book. The constant inquiry into when my book would come out helped motivate me to "just do it".

At the end of the day most importantly I acknowledge my partner, photographer and soul mate, Herman whose unwavering support, love and encouragement has motivated me to make this project a reality.

The Beginning

It all began in New York City almost thirty years ago when I started to work for a family friend with a successful catering business that needed extra help in her kitchen. I worked out of her loft in the twenties off Eighth Avenue and cooked everything from beignets to crème brulee. We worked many hours and catered all kinds of parties and from there my "career" in the food business took off. Fairly soon I was working with all the top caterers in Manhattan (including Martha Stewart for a few events) and went from cooking in alleyways in the pouring rain to catering parties for hundreds of people at the Met. It was a five year period of doing all the grunt work and loving it. I was busy, meeting a lot of people in the business and making invaluable contacts for my future in food.

I had never planned on a career in food or to become a chef. Cooking schools were unheard of back then and no one was professionally trained. You got a job, you worked you way up and the next thing you know you were head chef in some restaurant or catering business. My path took me to the kitchens of Ladies Home Journal, Food and Wine and Country Living magazines. I was a recipe tester before becoming a recipe developer and had joined a prestigious group of New York women who had formed a group called The New York Women's Culinary Alliance. I met Julia Child, Jacques Pepin and attended many events with Sarah Moulton. Back then there were no "celebrity chefs" and we were all equal; working hard and enjoying the food business in a very down to earth way.

I eventually opened my own catering business and did parties all over the Tri-state area with clients such as Ralph Lauren, Paul Simon and Diana Ross. I continued to write recipes for various magazines and had started my journey towards the health and wellness sector of the food world. I wrote hundreds of recipes for the Time/Life Fitness series of cookbooks and contributed regularly to Cooking Light, Food and Wine and Vegetarian Times. My clients continually requested low-fat and "healthier" foods and I learned to cook without all the butter and cream that many chefs rely on for flavor. I discovered fresh herbs, olive oil and stocks as a replacement for the traditional heavy sauce ingredients.

I eventually moved to Miami Beach in search of a healthier life style and began teaching at small local cooking schools with a focus on tropical ingredients. I was featured in The Miami Herald for my private in home cooking classes which were becoming very popular. After two years I discovered Miami was not challenging enough for me in many areas and the food business was quite limited. I began to feel the need to get back to New York so I packed up and drove North.

When I returned to Manhattan I was immediately employed by Peter Kump's New York Cooking School. I taught thousands of classes over a period of eleven years and watched the school grow from a small funky brownstone on the Upper East Side of Manhattan to what it is today. It is now a six floor state of the art nationally recognized institution that cranks out some of the best new chefs in the industry. I taught one of the first classes being offered where we had portable burners, no hot water or electricity and the temperature was over 80 degrees outside. It was quite the journey and well worth it. Today, I continue to travel to Manhattan to teach at one of my favorite schools in the New York area which was re-named The Institute of Culinary Education in the nineties.

I moved to the West coast in 2002 to pursue a more nature oriented lifestyle and have not looked back. For someone in the food business Southern California is a dream come true, incredible farmer's markets, access to local ranches and vineyards and the ability to grow your own garden year round is the perfect combination for me.

I have been teaching what I love for over twenty five years and have often been asked why I don't have a cookbook. I always came up with the reason of not having time or not knowing how to start or thinking it was already an over-saturated market. Who needs another cookbook, right?

After being asked by my students time and time again, I thought, now is the time to put together a book that expresses my idea of food and what I have been teaching for all these years. Contemporary healthy food that delights the taste buds and leaves you with a feeling of satisfaction each time you make a meal. You only need a few ingredients for most recipes and many dishes can be changed by adding a different spice or flavoring such as turning an Asian recipe into a Provencal one by leaving out cilantro and adding basil.

I have always enjoyed eating locally grown produce and in recent years have shopped for organic foods exclusively. It is important for health and flavor, to seek out un-adulterated, farm raised proteins and vegetables. I will not write the word "organic" into each recipe trusting that you will choose the best available ingredients you can find.

As the world grows smaller we all have various ethnic markets and restaurants in our neighborhoods. It is my aim to have you, the reader, try new cuisines at home simply by becoming more familiar with the various ingredients at these markets.

Cooking is a creative experience; you can change the recipe and make it yours, if you don't like cilantro use parsley, if the salmon isn't so fresh use halibut instead. Relax and enjoy the process of making a tasty and healthy meal that takes very little time and can be as creative as you want it to be.

I offer all kinds of tips throughout Simple Real Food. I suggest substitutes and include make-ahead recipes that can be done the day before or a month ahead and frozen.

Most of all I want the reader to come away with the desire to get in there and cook, to try new ingredients, and to realize that cooking can be easy, creative and fun.

Setting Up Your Kitchen

I am a big fan of simple and straightforward kitchens. I feel a smaller kitchen is actually more efficient and easier to work in because you can go from counter to stove in a shorter amount of time. Therefore I believe in less stuff. You need a few key items to set up your kitchen properly and to help create a comfortable space to cook in.

A large wood or heavy plastic cutting board is essential, you need enough room on it to be able to chop a few different things at once and not have to clear it off in between. I recommend a 14 by 10-inch board as well as at least one other smaller one so you can have someone else prepping at the same time or to switch to an alternate board just for proteins. A few very good knives are also crucial and I chose Wusthof, Henckels or Shun for my kitchen. There are many other knives that are also great so I recommend you to go to a store with kitchen tools and try out different knives. You are looking for a comfortable knife that is not too large for you but also has a good weight and is at least eight inches in length. The only knives you will need for a basic kitchen are a chef's knife, a paring knife and a bread knife. If you find that you are cooking a lot and start to butcher meat or slice fish you may also want a slicing or boning knife. But start with those three and you will be fine.

As far as equipment goes, you will want to invest in very good quality pots and pans. I am not going to go into all the name brands here but shop around and once again feel the weight of the pans and talk to the sales associate and find out what suits your needs and budget. It is just like any business where you have equipment that aids you in your work, the more you spend on the right equipment the higher the quality and the longer it will last I do enjoy a couple gadgets but in general I am not a fan of cluttering up your kitchen with a lot of stuff you won't use. With that in mind I recommend a food processor, immersion blender, electric mixer and spice grinder. That is about all I use on a regular basis so other gadgets would be not be on my personal must have list. I use tongs all the time for just about everything and recommend a number of pairs in varying sizes. Wooden spoons, rubber spatulas, measuring spoons and cups are all basic tools that you will need.

I have often consulted with clients of mine to build a kitchen or re-organize an existing one and the main factor is to use the space efficiently and have plenty of storage for platters, bowls, baking sheets and spices. No matter what size you have to work with a kitchen should always be a place you feel happy being in and that inspires you to cook.

Essentials: Ingredients

I have taught many classes that help people set up their kitchen properly and recommend staples to have on hand. This is an important step because it is the difference between making a meal or not. Often I hear people say that they have no time to shop and cook at the end of the day so why bother. Why not just take home food from the local market or restaurant? I believe that simple food that is delicious and quick to make is easily accessible and worth the effort. If you have the suggested staples on hand cooking can become part of your daily routine.

Here is the list:

* **Refrigerated items:** onions, garlic, celery, carrots, Dijon mustard, ketchup, capers, grated parmesan, unsalted butter, olives, tomato paste, anchovy paste, sesame oil and chutneys or relishes.

* **In the cupboard:** chicken broth, vegetable broth, a variety of rice, pasta, flour, canned tomatoes, olive oil, canola oil, vegetable cooking spray, vinegars, sugar, soy sauce, canned beans, canned tuna, honey, lentils, spices, kosher salt, fresh pepper and a couple of "emergency" dried herbs such as oregano and thyme.

With the above items you can prepare a simple meal at any time and will not have to go to the market. Or you can pick up a piece of fish or chicken and a vegetable on the way home and dinner will be on the table in half an hour.

Exotic or slightly harder to find ingredients will often be listed in the ingredient part of my recipes because I use many ethnic flavors in my cooking. I give alternatives for these ingredients in case you don't have access to a gourmet store in your area.

Read on and you will be motivated to cook with the greatest of ease and remember simpler is always better.

Appetizers

I think appetizer parties are one of the best ways to entertain, similar to tapas or dim sum, appetizers are small tastes of a variety of dishes that can be served hot, cold or room temperature.

Many of the recipes I have included in this section can be made ahead and frozen for easy party planning. It is important to remember to include different types of flavors, textures, colors and mode of preparation when choosing your menu.

I also suggest you keep in mind that at many parties there are vegetarians who need to have a few items to choose from so always include recipes that are without meat, fish, chicken and even dairy.

Lastly I recommend you plan a party according to what you may be serving after. If you are going to have dinner, two appetizers is sufficient and only make enough to last for half an hour otherwise your guests will be full before they get to the table. If you plan on a party that is just appetizers you will need at least five to six varieties and they should include meat, fish and chicken. In this case you will also need to make enough to last for three hours as this is the typical length of a cocktail party. With that in mind I suggest three appetizers per person of each item.

A well planned party is the key, choose a menu that is not going to keep you in the kitchen at the last minute. The make ahead tips I offer throughout the book will help you to entertain with ease and actually enjoy having guests.

Recipes

Hoisin Ginger Chicken with Mango Mayonnaise

This recipe makes 25 to 30 skewers

Preparation time: 10 minutes

Marinating time: 1 hour

Cooking time: 7 minutes

Ingredients

1/3 cup hoisin sauce

1 teaspoon toasted sesame oil

3 cloves garlic, minced

1 Tablespoon minced ginger

2 Tablespoons soy sauce

3 Tablespoons rice wine vinegar

2 whole, boneless, skinless, chicken breasts cut into 1-inch cubes

25 to 30 bamboo skewers

Mango Sauce:

1/4 cup mango chutney

1 lime, juiced

1/3 cup mayonnaise

2 Tablespoons cilantro, chopped

1 Tablespoon black and white sesame seeds, toasted, garnish

Procedure

1. Combine hoisin sauce, sesame oil, garlic, ginger, soy sauce, and rice vinegar in a medium bowl and add the chicken. Turn to coat and marinate at least 1 hour or up to overnight, refrigerated.

2. Heat the oven to 400. Meanwhile, make the dipping sauce.

3. Combine the mango chutney, lime juice, mayonnaise and cilantro in a food processor and puree. Transfer the puree to a small serving bowl. This sauce can be made in a blender or by hand by finely chopping the chutney and combining.

4. Skewer the chicken lengthwise two pieces to a skewer keeping the points covered and place on two baking sheets. Bake until cooked through about 7 minutes. Serve on a platter sprinkled with the toasted sesame seeds and the dipping sauce.

Make ahead tip: The chicken skewers can be made ahead up to the cooking step and frozen. Wrap the entire baking sheet in plastic wrap and freeze for up to 3 months. Defrost in the refrigerator overnight. Cook as above.

Alternatives: The chicken can be substituted with large cleaned shrimp, pork tenderloin, flank steak (cut thinly against the grain) sea scallops or firm tofu. If you would like to have a sauce without mayonnaise simple remove it and add a third a cup more of the chutney.

Sesame Seared Tuna on Wonton Crisps with Wasabi Crème Fraiche

This recipe makes 30 pieces

Preparation time: 15 minutes

Marinating time: 20 minutes

Cooking time: 25 minutes

Ingredients

1 piece Ahi grade tuna, 3/4 pound, cut into log shapes about 4 inches long by 1 1/2 inches wide

1/4 cup toasted sesame oil

3 Tablespoons soy sauce

1 cup sesame seeds, black and white, toasted in a dry skillet until golden

1/4 package square wonton skins

Canola oil for sautéing

1/2 ripe papaya, peeled, seeded, cut into thin 1/4-inch pieces

Chives, snipped, garnish

Wasabi Crème Fraiche:

1/2 cup crème fraiche, sour cream or mayonnaise

2 teaspoons wasabi powder

Salt, to taste

Procedure

1. Place the tuna in a bowl and coat with the sesame oil and soy sauce. Marinate about 20 minutes and no longer than one hour.

2. Place the sesame seeds on a baking sheet and coat the tuna logs with them, turning on all sides.

3. Heat a sauté pan over high heat. Lightly brush with canola oil. Sauté the tuna for 2 to 3 minutes on each side. Remove to a cutting board and slice thickly against the grain, then cut into cubes

small enough to fit onto the wonton triangles.

4. Meanwhile, cut the wontons into triangles. Heat enough oil to come up the side of a medium saucepan by 4 inches. When it is hot but not smoking fry the wontons a few at a time for about 30 seconds. They should be golden brown, if the oil is too hot lower the heat and allow it to cool a bit. Drain on paper towels.

5. For the sauce; in a small bowl combine the crème fraiche, wasabi and salt to taste. Mix well and adjust wasabi adding more if desired.

6. Top the wonton triangles with a cube of tuna and spoon a dollop of the wasabi crème on each piece of tuna.

7. Garnish each triangle with a sliver of papaya and a sprinkling of chives.

Make ahead tip: You can marinate and cook the tuna in the morning, fry the wonton skins a day before (store in a plastic container) and make the sauce up to 2 days ahead. Prep the papaya and chives the day before if desired. When the guests arrive you can slice the tuna and assemble.

Alternatives: You can use round rice crackers in place of the wontons to save time and replace the tuna with salmon, if desired. Cook the salmon for about 5 minutes on each side and proceed as above.

Skewered Beef or Chicken Satay with Spicy Peanut Sauce

This recipe makes 30

Preparation time: 30 minutes

Marinating time: 2 hours

Cooking time: 7 minutes

Ingredients

1 flank steak, cut into thin strips against the grain or 1 1/2 pounds boneless, skinless chicken breasts, cut into chunks

1/3 cup lime juice

3 teaspoons minced ginger

3 cloves garlic, minced

1 jalapeno pepper, seeded, minced

1/3 cup soy sauce

1/4 cup canola oil

Peanut Sauce:

1/2 cup smooth natural peanut butter

3 Tablespoons soy sauce

3 Tablespoons lime juice

2 cloves garlic, peeled, halved

1/4 to 1/2 teaspoons red pepper flakes

1 Tablespoons minced ginger

3 Tablespoons chopped cilantro

Water, as needed

Procedure

1. Skewer the beef or if using chicken use two pieces per skewer. Place on two baking sheets.

Combine the remaining ingredients in a small bowl and then pour over the beef. Marinate at least 2 hours at room temperature or overnight refrigerated.

2. Heat the oven to 400. Thirty minutes before cooking remove the skewers from the refrigerator.

3. Combine the sauce ingredients in a food processor and process until smooth. Thin with water until it is the consistency of a dipping sauce. Transfer to a small serving bowl.

4. Cook the skewers about 5 to 7 minutes.

5. Serve the skewers on a platter with the dipping sauce in the center.

Make ahead tip: You can make the skewers up to the cooking step, wrap the baking sheets with plastic wrap and freeze for up to 3 months. Defrost overnight in the refrigerator before baking. The sauce can be frozen in a plastic container for up to 3 months. Heat lighly before serving adding more water if the texture is too thick.

Alternatives: You can use shrimp, scallops, pork tenderloin or firm tofu in place of the chicken or beef.

Corn Cakes with Smoked Salmon and Crème Fraiche

This recipe makes 35

Preparation time: 30 minutes

Cooking time: 15 minutes

Ingredients

1, 10 oz. package frozen corn, defrosted

2 cloves garlic

2 teaspoons Tabasco

3 scallions, roughly chopped

2 eggs

1/2 cup flour

1/2 cup chopped parsley or cilantro

1 teaspoon salt

Fresh pepper, to taste

Canola oil

5 oz. thinly sliced smoked salmon

Crème fraiche

3 Tablespoons chives, snipped, garnish

Procedure

1. Combine the corn, garlic, Tabasco and scallions in a food processor and puree. Transfer to a bowl and stir in the eggs, flour, parsley, salt and pepper.

2. Heat a large skillet and add a thin layer of oil. Add a tablespoon of the batter to test one cake to make sure it is seasoned to taste. Sauté until golden about 3 or 4 minutes on each side. Drain on paper towels.

3. Re-season if necessary and continue with all the batter. Keep warm in a 200 oven.

4. To serve, arrange the corn cakes on a serving tray and top with a small piece of smoked salmon a tiny dollop of crème fraiche and garnish with the chives. Serve warm.

Make ahead tip: The batter can be made ahead and either frozen for three months or refrigerated for up to a week. Or you can make the cakes completely ahead and refrigerate for the same time. To re-heat arrange the defrosted corn cakes in one layer on baking sheets and warm in a 300 oven for 10 minutes and proceed with the recipe.

Alternatives: You can omit the salmon if you have vegetarian guests and use a sprinkling of finely diced red pepper instead, for color. Chick peas can be used in place of the corn for chick pea cakes.

Vegetable Samosas

This recipe makes 30

Preparation time: 30 minutes

Cooking time: 10 minutes

Ingredients

1 teaspoon chopped ginger

2 cloves garlic, minced

1 teaspoon coriander seeds

1/2 teaspoon peppercorns

2 Tablespoons canola oil

1 yam, peeled, finely diced

4 scallions, thinly sliced

1 cup corn kernels

1 teaspoon curry powder

2 Tablespoons soy sauce

1 teaspoon sugar

1 package wonton skins

2 Tablespoons cornstarch mixed with 4 Tablespoons cold water

Soy Dipping Sauce:

1/4 cup soy sauce

2 Tablespoons rice vinegar

2 teaspoons sugar

2 Tablespoons lime juice

2 cloves garlic, minced

1 teaspoon minced ginger

1 jalapeno, seeded, minced

1 scallion, thinly sliced

Canola oil, for frying

Procedure

1. Combine the garlic and ginger and set aside. Grind the coriander and peppercorns in a spice grinder.

2. Heat the oil in a large skillet and sauté the garlic, ginger, and spices for 30 seconds. Add the remaining vegetables, curry, soy and sugar and cook stirring for 5 minutes. Set aside to cool.

3. Place a wonton skin on your work surface. Dip your finger into the cornstarch mixture and spread a little on the edges of the skin and then fill with a scant tablespoon of the filling. Fold over to make a triangle and press edges to seal.

4. Heat enough oil to come up 1/2 way in a medium saucepan until hot but not smoking.

5. Meanwhile make the dipping sauce. Combine the ingredients in a small saucepan and bring to a simmer, taste and adjust seasoning. Transfer to a small serving bowl.

6. To test the oil for the correct frying heat; drop a samosa into the oil and if it cooks quickly it is ready. Fry the samosas in batches until golden, about 2 minutes, drain on paper towels. If the oil gets too hot and the samosas turn overly brown turn off the heat and allow the oil to cool before continuing to fry the samosas.

7. Serve with the soy dipping sauce.

Make ahead tip: You can make all the samosas ahead up to step six and freeze on a baking sheet lined with parchment paper. After they are frozen they can be transferred to a plastic bag. Cook them frozen until golden brown and crispy about 2 to 3 minutes.

Alternatives: Use diced white potato in place of the yam add 1/4 pound ground lamb or chicken along with the other ingredients for a meat samosa.

Crostini with Herbed Chèvre and Caramelized Onions

This recipe makes 30

Preparation time: 30 minutes

Cooking time: 10 minutes.

Ingredients

1 baguette, thinly sliced

Olive oil for brushing

2 cloves garlic, halved

8 oz. chevre, room temperature

2 teaspoons chopped rosemary

1 Tablespoon chopped thyme

Salt, pepper to taste

1/4 cup olive oil

Onions:

1 Tablespoon butter

1 1/2 pounds red onions, thinly sliced

1 1/2 Tablespoons sugar

1 teaspoon thyme, chopped

2 Tablespoons sherry wine or balsamic vinegar

Salt and pepper

Rosemary sprigs, garnish

Procedure

1. Heat oven to 400. Brush the bread lightly with the olive oil and toast in the oven until lightly browned about 8 minutes. Rub the crostini with the cut sides of the garlic. Discard garlic.

2. Combine the chevre with the herbs, salt, pepper and olive oil in a small bowl. Mash it up with the back of a fork. Set aside.

3. In a large skillet over medium low heat melt the butter. Add the onions, sugar and thyme and cook, stirring occasionally until the onions are very soft and brown about 25 minutes. Increase the heat to high and add the vinegar. Cook until the vinegar is evaporated about 2 minutes, season to taste with salt and pepper and set aside to cool.

4. Spread the herbed cheese liberally on the toasts.

5. Spoon a dollop of onions onto each crostini and garnish with rosemary sprigs.

Make ahead tip: You can make the toasts and store them in a plastic bag for 2 days. The chevre and onions can also be made 2 days ahead and stored in the refrigerator. Allow all the components to come to room temperature before assembling.

Alternatives: You can use shredded mozzarella or parmesan in place of the chevre, heat the toasts with the cheese on top before garnishing with the onions and rosemary. You can also use pesto in place of the onions if desired.

Thai Summer Rolls with Lime Dipping Sauce

This recipe makes 10

Preparation time: 40 minutes

Cooking time: 5 minutes

Ingredients

3/4 pound large shrimp, peeled, de-veined, cooked

8 leaves red leaf lettuce

1 package small spring roll skins, 8-inch rounds (also known as rice paper wrappers)

1/2 English cucumber, seeded, julienne

1 red pepper, seeded, julienne

2 ripe avocados cut into thin slices

1/2 cup packed cilantro leaves, rinsed, dried

1/2 cup packed mint leaves, rinsed, dried

1/2 cup packed basil leaves, rinsed, dried

Lime Dipping Sauce:

1 teaspoon red pepper flakes

Juice of 3 limes

1/4 cup fish sauce

3 Tablespoons sugar

1 Tablespoon minced garlic

Procedure

1. Slice the shrimp in half lengthwise. Set aside.
2. Pull the leaves off the lettuce and separate into large chunks removing the white inner core. Set

aside.

3. Soak a few wrappers at a time in warm water until pliable. Make sure to remove the wrappers when they are soft and pliable and place on a baking sheet lined with paper towels.

4. Working with one wrapper at a time place a piece of lettuce on the lower edge of the wrapper leaving enough room on the sides to fold in. Place 2 shrimp halves on the lettuce, top with a piece of cucumber, red pepper, avocado, a few leaves of cilantro, mint and basil. Roll the filling to the middle pulling the mixture towards you tightly to cover the filling completely. When you get to the center fold the sides in and continue rolling to the end. The end will adhere to the other side of the wrapper. Place seam side down on a baking sheet until they are all finished.

5. Combine all the ingredients for the sauce in a small saucepan and simmer for 3 or 4 minutes to dissolve the sugar. Transfer to a serving bowl.

6. Cut the rolls on the diagonal and serve with the dipping sauce.

Make ahead tip: You can make the rolls and sauce completely ahead and store wrapped well with plastic wrap for up to 5 hours for the rolls and a week for the sauce.

Alternatives: You can substitute firm tofu for the shrimp – drained, pressed dry and finely diced then marinated in 1 tablespoon sesame oil and 1 tablespoon soy sauce. Cooked, drained ground pork or chicken can also be used. Sauté the pork or ground chicken in 1 tablespoon of canola oil and add a tablespoon of fish or soy sauce before removing from the heat.

COLUMBIA
HOTELS & RESORTS

(860)

227-8128

Cell ?

Spicy Crab Cakes with Chipotle Mayonnaise

This recipe makes 30 crab cakes

Preparation time: 30 minutes

Cooking time: 10 minutes

Chilling time: 30 minutes

Ingredients

1 Tablespoon canola oil, plus more for crab cakes

1 small onion, minced

2 cloves garlic, minced

2 scallions, thinly sliced

1 jalapeno, seeded, minced

3 Tablespoons chopped cilantro

2 eggs

1/2 cup mayonnaise

1 cup breadcrumbs

1 pound lump crab meat, picked over for cartilage

Salt, pepper

2 Tablespoons Dijon mustard

1 1/2 cups Panko breadcrumbs, for coating the crab cakes

Chipotle Mayonnaise:

1 chipotle pepper

1/2 cup mayonnaise

1 Tablespoon lime juice

Salt, pepper, to taste

Procedure

1. In a medium skillet heat the oil and sauté the onion until softened about 3 minutes. Add garlic, scallions and jalapeno and cook another 2 minutes, season with salt and pepper. Set aside.

2. Combine cilantro, eggs, mayonnaise, breadcrumbs, crab meat, salt, pepper and mustard in a medium bowl. Add onion mixture and mix well. Shape into one inch cakes and place on a baking sheet coated with a thin layer of panko. Toss the cakes in the bread crumbs. Chill for about 30 minutes.

3. Meanwhile make the sauce; combine all the ingredients in a processor and blend until smooth, taste and adjust seasoning. Transfer to a small bowl and chill.

4. Heat a large skillet over medium heat; add a thin layer of canola oil and sauté the crab cakes until golden on both sides, about 3 minutes per side. Transfer to paper towels to drain.

5. Arrange the cakes on a serving platter and spoon a dollop of the mayonnaise on each crab cake before serving.

Make ahead tip: The crab cakes can be made ahead completely and frozen wrapped well with plastic wrap for up to 3 months. They can also be made up to where they are formed but are not cooked yet and frozen. To defrost, set in the refrigerator overnight or cook frozen the same as above. If you want to sauté them ahead they can be re-heated on a baking sheet for 10 minutes in a 300 oven.

Alternatives: You can substitute a ripe avocado for the chipotle you can also leaving out the mayonnaise. Mash the avocado until smooth add a tablespoon of lime juice, a tablespoon of chopped cilantro, salt and pepper to taste.

Shrimp and Ginger Pot Stickers with Soy Dipping Sauce

This recipe makes 30

Preparation time: 40 minutes

Cooking time: 10 minutes

Ingredients

1/2 pound large shrimp, peeled, de-veined or 1/2 pound ground pork

1 egg white

1 teaspoon chili oil

1 teaspoon toasted sesame oil

1 Tablespoon soy sauce

1 carrot, peeled, grated finely

1 cup finely chopped cabbage

1 Tablespoon grated ginger

1 shallot, minced

1 Tablespoon cilantro, chopped, plus whole leaves for garnish

Fresh pepper

1 package round wonton skins

Cornstarch

Soy Dipping Sauce:

1/3 cup soy sauce

1 teaspoon toasted sesame oil

2 Tablespoons rice wine vinegar

2 scallions, thinly sliced

1/4 teaspoon red pepper flakes

Canola oil for sautéing

Procedure

1. Combine the shrimp, egg white, chili oil, sesame oil and soy sauce in a food processor and process 1 minute to form a paste. Transfer to a medium bowl and add the carrot, cabbage, ginger, shallot, chopped cilantro and pepper. Mix well. If using ground pork, skip the processor and combine all the ingredients in a medium bowl.

2. Place a heaping teaspoon in the center of each wrapper and moisten the edges with a little water. Seal and make sure the dumplings stand. Place on a tray with parchment or wax paper and continue with the remaining filling and wonton wrappers.

3. Combine the sauce ingredients in a small bowl and set aside.

4. Heat a large non-stick skillet and coat lightly with canola oil. Place half the pot stickers in the skillet making sure they are standing and brown the bottoms about 2 to 3 minutes. Add 1/2 cup of hot water mixed with a tablespoon of cornstarch, cover for 5 minutes. Uncover and continue to cook until all the water is evaporated. Remove carefully with a spatula to a serving dish being careful not to rip the bottoms. Repeat with the other half of the pot stickers. Serve with the dipping sauce and cilantro leaves as a garnish.

Make ahead tip: The pot stickers can be made ahead and frozen on a baking sheet lightly coated with cornstarch or lined with parchment paper to prevent sticking. Remove from the freezer and place right into the hot skillet, do not defrost.

Alternatives: You can use ground chicken in place of the shrimp or drained finely diced firm tofu. If using tofu marinate for an hour in a tablespoon of soy sauce and 2 teaspoons of sesame oil.

Coconut Shrimp with Pineapple Apricot Dipping Sauce

This recipe serves 12

Preparation time: 40 minutes

Cooking time: 10 minutes

Chilling time: 1 hour

Ingredients

1 cup flour

3/4 teaspoon salt

1 teaspoon cayenne

5 egg whites, lightly beaten

2 1/2 cups shredded unsweetened coconut

1 1/2 pounds large shrimp, peeled, de-veined

2 cups canola oil, for frying

Pineapple Apricot Dipping Sauce:

1 cup canned unsweetened pineapple chunks drained

3 scallions, white part only, thinly sliced

1/4 cup apricot preserves

1/4 cup cilantro leaves

2 Tablespoons lime juice

1/2 jalapeno, roughly chopped

Salt, to taste

Procedure

1. Combine the flour, salt and cayenne on a flat baking sheet. Place the egg whites and shredded coconut on two separate plates. Dredge the shrimp in the flour mixture, egg whites, then coconut. Press the coconut onto the shrimp. Chill for at least an hour.

2. In a processor combine the pineapple, scallions, apricot preserves, cilantro, lime juice, jalapeno and salt to taste. Process until blended and taste, adjust seasoning. Transfer to a small serving dish.

3. Heat the oven to 200. In a medium saucepan heat the oil until moderately hot but not smoking. Working in batches; fry the shrimp until golden about 2 minutes and then drain on a paper towel lined baking sheet. Transfer to the oven to keep warm.

4. Serve the hot shrimp on a platter with the dipping sauce.

Make ahead tip: You can make the shrimp up to the cooking step and freeze them for up to 3 months. Cook them directly from the freezer, do not defrost.

Alternatives: You can use boneless, skinless chicken breasts cut into 1-inch chunks in place of the shrimp. If you don't like cilantro, flat leaf parsley can be used instead. For a milder sauce omit the jalapeno.

Salads and Dressings

I often think of salad as a main course and I enjoy it for an entrée on a regular basis. Salads can be simple or elegant, dressed up or down, as an accent to a meal or a stunning main course. For me a salad is a must have as part of a menu for any type of meal.

The main thing to focus on with salads is freshness of ingredients. You can make the loveliest salad with a simple fresh head of baby lettuce, a drizzle of good olive oil and a squeeze of lemon juice. So the important thing to remember is use the freshest ingredients and use dressing sparingly. There is nothing more un-appealing then a salad drowning in vinaigrette.

One of the ingredients for a great dressing is a high quality olive oil. Italians are the best at making olive oil since it is a main export of theirs, but California, France, Turkey and Greece all have delicious olive oils, worth trying. The main thing is to try different ones and decide what you like. Cooking with extra virgin or virgin olive oil is not the best use of the oil - I prefer canola or grape seed oil which holds the heat well and doesn't over-power the dish.

Vinegars of many varieties are also important; one should have a good quality balsamic, sherry wine, red wine, rice wine and once in a while try something new such as Champagne or garlic vinegar. I am often asked about the quality of balsamic vinegar and what the differences are and I have one answer to that; you get what you pay for. So it is important to try different quality vinegars to see for yourself. The proof is in the tasting and there is quite a gap between supermarket brands and something you might find at a local gourmet store.

Fresh herbs are terrific in salads. I use basil, mint, chives, tarragon, dill, cilantro and flat leaf parsley regularly to flavor my vinaigrettes. Here is where the most important ingredient comes in; you have to make your own dressing! It takes all of 5 minutes and makes the world of difference in a salad no matter how simple. If you only have two minutes, use fresh lemon or lime and olive oil and you have a dressing. I never recommend bottled dressing, no matter what the circumstances are.

I also suggest you assemble your salad ahead and dress it right before it comes to the table. Serve it only slightly chilled as cold salads are less flavorful and remember a little dressing goes a long way, you can always add more.

The following chapter is mainly comprised of Entrée salads - these are served as a main course and are often arranged. This means you have a beautiful platter and you set the ingredients on the platter in a colorful arrangement, passing the dressing on the side

I also included a few side or appetizer salads which are tossed before serving and can be individually plated.

Simpler is always better with side salads so resist the temptation to add everything from the refrigerator to the salad bowl. A few ingredients simply dressed create an elegant and delicious salad course.

Salads and Dressings

Asian Chicken Salad with Sesame Cilantro Dressing ...37

Caesar Salad...39

Nicoise Salad with Grilled Tuna...41

Arugula Watercress Salad with Lemon Vinaigrette...43

Warm Beet Salad with Chevre and Candied Walnuts...44

Chicken and Apple Salad with Citrus Vinaigrette...46

Grilled Seafood Salad with Lemon Dressing...48

Thai Shrimp Salad with Asian Dressing...50

Asian Chicken Salad with Sesame Cilantro Dressing

Serves 6

Preparation time: 25 minutes

Cooking time: 10 minutes

Ingredients

2 whole, boneless, skinless chicken breasts, trimmed, halved

3 cups low sodium chicken broth

1 red pepper, halved, seeded, julienne

1 small jicama, peeled, julienne

1/2 pound snow peas, trimmed, blanched

2 cloves garlic, minced

2 teaspoons minced ginger

1/2 cup soy sauce

2 Tablespoons rice vinegar

2 teaspoons brown sugar

3 Tablespoons canola oil

2 teaspoons toasted sesame oil

3 Tablespoons chopped cilantro

1/4 pound bean sprouts

3 scallions, julienne, garnish

2 Tablespoons toasted sesame seeds, garnish

Procedure

1. Place the chicken in a large skillet cover with the broth and bring to a simmer over medium heat. Simmer until cooked through about 6 to 8 minutes. Remove to a plate and allow to cool.

2. Combine the red pepper, jicama and snow peas in a large bowl. Cut the chicken into thin strips

and add to the bowl.

3. In a small bowl combine the garlic, ginger, soy, vinegar, sugar, canola and sesame oils and cilantro. Whisk and taste for seasoning.

4. Pour the dressing over the chicken salad and toss gently. Spoon the salad onto a large serving platter and top with the bean sprouts, scallions and toasted sesame seeds. Serve at room temperature.

Make ahead tip: You can make the salad and dressing up to 2 days ahead. Simply toss the dressing with the main ingredients a half an hour before serving.

Alternatives: You can use poached or grilled turkey breast, shrimp or sea scallops in place of the chicken and substitute flat leaf parsley for the cilantro.

Caesar Salad

Serves 4

Preparation time: 20 minutes

Cooking time: 8 minutes

Ingredients

1 head romaine lettuce, washed, torn into pieces, dried

1/4 baguette

Olive oil

Salt and pepper

1 large egg*

2 cloves garlic, peeled

Juice of 1 lemon

1 Tablespoon Worcestershire sauce

3 anchovies

3/4 cup extra virgin olive oil

1/3 cup grated parmesan cheese

Shaved parmesan, garnish

Procedure

1. Place the lettuce in a bowl and refrigerate.

2. Heat the oven to 400.

3. Cut the baguette into small quarter-inch cubes. Toss in a bowl with olive oil, salt and pepper. Spread out on a baking sheet and toast until golden, about 10 minutes. Remove and set aside.

4. Combine the egg, garlic, lemon juice, Worcestershire sauce and anchovies in a processor and process about 1 minute. Add oil slowly thru the feed tube while the machine is running. Add the cheese, salt and pepper to taste and process. Taste and adjust seasoning.

5. Toss about half of the dressing with the lettuce.

6. Arrange the lettuce on four plates. Top with the croutons, shaved cheese and extra dressing if desired.

Make ahead tip: You can make the dressing and croutons at least 3 days ahead.

Alternatives: For chicken Caesar use 1 1/2 pounds boneless skinless chicken breast, pounded thin and marinated in 1/4 cup olive oil, juice of 1 lemon, salt and pepper and grill for 4 minutes on each side. Slice and serve over the salad. You can also use large shrimp in place of the chicken; follow the same procedure as the chicken, cooking the shrimp for 2 minutes per side.

*The lemon in the dressing helps to "cook" the raw egg so it is safe to eat.

Nicoise Salad with Grilled Tuna

Serves 8

Preparation time: 30 minutes

Cooking time: 10 minutes

Ingredients

1 Tablespoon Dijon mustard

2 cloves minced garlic

3 Tablespoons Balsamic vinegar

1/2 cup extra virgin olive oil

Salt, pepper

1 pound new potatoes, washed and quartered

12 oz. haricot verts or green beans, stem ends trimmed

3 large eggs

2 tuna steaks, about 8 oz. each or 2 cans water packed tuna, drained and crumbled

Olive oil

Lettuce for platter

2 ripe tomatoes cut into eighths

10 Nicoise olives

4 anchovies, rinsed and drained, optional

6 basil leaves, chiffonade *

Procedure

1. Combine the mustard, vinegar and garlic in a bowl and whisk, add oil slowly while whisking, season with salt and pepper. Set aside.

2. Cover potatoes in a small saucepan with cold water adding a pinch of salt. Cook until tender about 20 minutes, drain, set aside.

3. Blanch the beans in boiling salted water, refresh with cold water, set aside.

4. Place eggs in a small saucepan of cold water and bring to a boil, remove from heat, cover for 15 minutes. Rinse with cold water and then peel the eggs and cut into quarters.

5. Meanwhile rub the tuna with olive oil, salt and pepper. Heat the grill and grill for 2 to 3 minutes on each side. Remove to a cutting board.

6. Arrange lettuce on a large serving platter; arrange the different groups of vegetables in piles around the platter. Slice tuna in half-inch slices and add to the platter. Scatter with olives, lay anchovies on top and sprinkle basil over the whole platter. Drizzle the dressing over the platter before serving. Serve cold or room temperature.

- For chiffonade roll the leaves into a log shape and then cut across the end

Make ahead tip: The entire salad can be made ahead and arranged the day you serve it up to 1 day before. The eggs can be hard boiled 4 days ahead and the haricot verts can be blanched 2 days ahead and reserved in a plastic bag in the refrigerator.

Alternatives: Boneless, skinless chicken breast, salmon or halibut can be used in place of the tuna. Simply grill the same way but for 4 minutes on each side.

Arugula, Watercress Salad with Lemon Vinaigrette

Serves 6

Preparation time: 15 minutes

Ingredients

2 bunches arugula, stems removed washed and spun dry

2 bunches watercress, tough stems removed

1 lemon, juiced

1 Tablespoon Dijon mustard

1/3 to 1/2 cup extra virgin olive oil

2 Tablespoons chopped herbs such as parsley, basil, cilantro, mint or tarragon

Salt, pepper

Procedure

1. Combine the arugula and watercress in a large bowl and toss.
2. Combine the lemon and Dijon in a small bowl and whisk; add the oil slowly while whisking, season to taste with salt, pepper and herbs.
3. Toss some of the dressing with the greens and reserve any leftover dressing for another salad.

Make ahead tip: You can wash and dry the greens and place in a serving bowl in the refrigerator in the morning. The dressing can be made ahead and kept for up to 10 days refrigerated, if making ahead add the herbs before serving.

Alternatives: Use any green lettuce you like in place of the watercress or arugula and remember not to chop the watercress, simple remove the stems near the top and leave in the whole leaf form. Any acid is fine in place of the lemon such as lime, orange or any type of vinegar.

Warm Beet Salad with Chèvre and Candied Walnuts

Serves 4

Preparation time: 30 minutes

Cooking time: 25 minutes

Ingredients

2 pounds beets, washed and quartered

Olive oil

Salt, pepper to taste

1 teaspoon lemon zest

1/2 cup fresh lemon juice

3 Tablespoons extra virgin olive oil

6 Tablespoons chopped mint

3 heads endive, sliced into thin julienne strips

1 bunch watercress, tough stems removed

5 oz. chevre

1/2 cup candied walnuts

Candied Walnuts:

1 cup walnuts

2 Tablespoons corn syrup

2 Tablespoons sugar

1/2 teaspoon salt

1/4 teaspoon pepper

Pinch of cayenne pepper or 1/2 teaspoon curry powder

Procedure

1. Heat the oven to 400. Place the beets on a baking sheet and toss with olive oil, salt and pepper. Roast until tender about 25 minutes. Remove from the oven and cool.

2. Meanwhile combine the lemon zest, lemon juice, olive oil, salt, pepper and mint in a large bowl and whisk. Taste and adjust seasoning. Reserve 3 tablespoons of the dressing in a medium bowl.

3. Heat the oven to 325. Spray a baking sheet with vegetable cooking spray. Toss the nuts with the corn syrup, sugar, salt, pepper and cayenne on the baking sheet and bake until nuts are caramelized about 15 minutes. Cool on the baking sheet. Break into pieces before serving.

4. Dice the beets and add to the reserved dressing, toss.

5. Add the endive and watercress to the larger bowl of dressing and toss well, arrange on four salad plates. Top with the beets and crumble the chevre over the top, sprinkle with some of the walnuts and serve warm or at room temperature.

Make ahead tip: You can make the dressing, beets and walnuts up to 3 days ahead. Assemble right before serving.

Alternatives: Use almonds, pecans or cashews in place of the walnuts or just omit altogether. You can substitute any salad greens you prefer and use feta cheese instead of chevre if desired.

Chicken and Apple Salad with Citrus Vinaigrette

Serves 4

Preparation time: 30 minutes

Cooking time: 40 minutes

Ingredients

1 whole, boneless, skinless chicken breast, halved

1 1/2 cups chicken broth

1/4 cup fresh orange juice

Salt, pepper, to taste

1 pink grapefruit, juiced

1 small shallot, minced

3 Tablespoons lemon juice

1/3 to 1/2 cup extra virgin olive oil

1 Granny Smith apple, peeled, cored, cut into thin strips

2 bunches watercress, tough stems removed

1/3 cup walnuts or pecans, toasted in a dry skillet for 3 minutes, roughly chopped

Procedure

1. In a medium skillet combine the chicken, chicken broth and orange juice, season with salt and pepper. Bring to a simmer over medium heat and simmer the chicken until it is cooked through about 5 to 8 minutes, remove to a plate and let cool.

2. Combine the grapefruit juice, shallot and lemon juice in a small bowl, whisk in the olive oil slowly, season with salt and pepper and set aside.

3. Cut the chicken into thin strips and transfer to a medium bowl. Add the apple and half the dressing, toss well.

4. Combine the watercress with the remaining dressing in a large bowl and toss. Mound the salad onto four large plates and top with the chicken and apples, garnish with the toasted nuts.

Make ahead tip: The salad can be prepared up to a day ahead without the dressing. Squeeze a lemon over the cut apple to prevent it from browning. Keep the watercress intact until ready to assemble. Toss all the components with the dressing a half an hour before serving.

Alternatives: You can poach turkey breast, shrimp or scallops if desired in place of the chicken. Any type of salad green such as endive, mixed greens, romaine or red leaf lettuce along with or in place of the watercress.

Grilled Seafood Salad with Lemon Dressing

Serves 6

Preparation time: 30 minutes

Cooking time: 10 minutes

Ingredients

4 Tablespoons lemon juice

1 Tablespoon Dijon mustard

2 garlic cloves, minced

1/2 cup extra virgin olive oil

Salt and pepper, to taste

6 basil leaves, chopped

Salad:

1 pound squid, cleaned cut into rounds, tentacles saved for another use or discarded

12 jumbo shrimp, peeled, de-veined, halved lengthwise

12 sea scallops, halved lengthwise

1 pound haricot verts, trimmed, cut into 2-inch lengths

Red leaf lettuce leaves

1 pint mixed yellow and red cherry tomatoes, halved

1 cup pitted Kalamata olives

Procedure

1. Combine the lemon, mustard and garlic in a small bowl and whisk. Add the oil, whisking slowly, Season with salt, pepper and basil. Set aside.

2. Combine the squid, shrimp and scallops in a large bowl and add 5 tablespoons of the dressing. Marinate at least 15 minutes.

3. Blanch the haricot verts in boiling salted water, drain, refresh. Transfer to a small bowl and add 3

tablespoons of the dressing.

4. Line a serving platter with the lettuce leaves.

5. Heat a grill pan over high heat. Grill the seafood for 2 to 3 minutes on each side. Arrange the grilled seafood on the lettuce with the haricot verts. Scatter the tomatoes and olives over the top and drizzle with any remaining dressing.

Make ahead tip: You can make the salad entirely the day before and assemble it right before you are serving. The dressing will last for a week in the refrigerator.

Alternatives: Other seafood can be used such as salmon, tuna, lobster or halibut. Marinate and grill as above. Snap peas, asparagus, snow peas or regular green beans can be substituted in place of the haricot verts.

Serves 4

Preparation time: 30 minutes

Cooking time: 5 minutes

Ingredients

1 pound large shrimp, peeled, de-veined

5 Tablespoons soy sauce

2 teaspoons toasted sesame oil

1 stalk lemongrass, minced

2 small carrots, peeled, julienne into 3-inch strips, blanched and refreshed

1/2 large European cucumber, seeded, julienne into 3 inch strips

2 cups thinly sliced red cabbage

3 Tablespoons rice wine vinegar

1 Tablespoon light brown sugar

1 Tablespoon roughly chopped ginger

1/4 teaspoon red pepper flakes

2 Tablespoons canola oil

3 Tablespoons cilantro, chopped

3 Tablespoons mint, chopped

1/4 cup dry roasted peanuts, roughly chopped

Procedure

1. Combine the shrimp with 2 tablespoons of the soy sauce, 1 teaspoon of the sesame oil and half the lemongrass. Marinate for 30 minutes or up to 2 hours.

2. Toss the carrots, cucumber and cabbage together in a large bowl.

3. Combine the vinegar, sugar, ginger, red pepper flakes, remaining lemongrass and soy sauce in the food processor. Add the canola and sesame oils slowly thru the feed tube. Stir in the cilantro and mint. Taste and adjust seasoning. Toss with the cabbage salad and set aside.

4. Heat a grilling pan until hot. Grill the shrimp 2 to 3 minutes on each side.

5. Arrange the salad on a serving platter surround with the shrimp and garnish with the nuts.

Make ahead tip: You can make the entire salad in the morning or the day before and serve at room temperature. Simply dress the salad right before serving.

Alternatives: Use scallops instead of shrimp and omit the peanuts if you wish.

Soups

Soup is a satisfying and simple meal to make with very little planning or special ingredients. You can clean out your refrigerator and sauté everything in a large saucepan, add broth and simmer it for thirty minutes and voila, you have soup. Either puree the ingredients with an immersion blender or food processor or leave chunky and flavor with whatever herbs and spices you may have and you will enjoy a hearty delicious dish. The ease of preparation makes soup a wonderful entree as well as a perfect first course. Another benefit to soup is most recipes can be made ahead and kept in the freezer for up to three months.

I recommend keeping the basic three ingredients needed to begin any soup on hand; celery, carrots and onion. From there; vegetables, meats, chicken or fish can be added to transform this simple dish to the most elegant entrée.

For all of the recipes here you can use vegetable broth in place of chicken or beef broth to make a vegetarian soup.

Remember that soup is not just meant for the winter months, cold soups are a wonderful and healthy way to enjoy your vegetables as well. Gazpacho is the perfect summer soup that can be enjoyed when it's too hot to cook or eat warm foods.

Recipes

Butternut Squash Soup with Ginger and Crème Fraiche

Serves 6

Preparation time: 30 minutes

Cooking time: 1 hour 5 minutes

Ingredients

1 large butternut squash halved, seeded

Olive oil for brushing

1 Tablespoon butter

2 leeks, white part only, thinly sliced

2 medium carrots, peeled, diced

2 celery stalks, diced

1 Tablespoon minced ginger

2 cloves garlic, minced

4 cups vegetable or chicken broth

Salt, pepper

1/3 cup crème fraiche

3 Tablespoons snipped chives, garnish

Procedure

1. Heat the oven to 375. Place the squash cut side down on a baking sheet coated lightly with olive oil. Roast until tender about 35 minutes.

2. Meanwhile melt the butter in a large saucepan and sauté the leeks, carrots, celery, ginger and garlic for 5 minutes over low heat. Season with salt and pepper to taste. Add the broth and bring to a boil, lower the heat to a simmer and cook for 15 minutes.

3. Remove the squash from the oven and allow to cool slightly. Scoop the flesh from the skin and add to the saucepan. Simmer for another 15 minutes.

4. Puree the soup in batches in a processor, taste for seasoning. Transfer back to the saucepan and heat through.

5. Spoon the soup into six soup bowls and spoon a small dollop of crème fraiche onto each serving, sprinkle with the chives and serve.

   Make ahead tip: You can make the recipe ahead and keep it in the refrigerator for up to 3 days. Or it can be frozen for 3 months.

   Alternatives: The butternut squash can be changed to acorn squash, zucchini or yellow squash. Yogurt or sour cream can be used in place of the crème fraiche if desired.

Gazpacho

Serves 8 to 10

Preparation time: 35 minutes

Cooking time: 10 minutes

Ingredients

1 red onion, minced

1 large cucumber, peeled, seeded, diced

1 red pepper, seeded, diced

1 yellow pepper, seeded, diced

3 large ripe tomatoes, seeded, chopped

3 stalks celery, finely diced

2 garlic cloves, minced

1/4 cup red or white wine vinegar

2 Tablespoons basil, chopped

2 Tablespoons flat leaf parsley, chopped

4 cups tomato juice or V-8 juice

Salt and pepper, to taste

2 teaspoons Tabasco

Homemade croutons, optional:

1 baguette, day old if possible

3 Tablespoons olive oil

Salt and pepper

Procedure

1. Combine the vegetables, vinegar, herbs, juice, salt, pepper and Tabasco in a large bowl, taste

and adjust seasoning.

2. For the croutons, heat the oven to 400. Cut the bread into small cubes and toss with the olive oil, salt and pepper in a large bowl. Transfer to a baking sheet and toast about 10 minutes. Store in an airtight container until ready to use.

3. Chill soup overnight if possible and serve with a few croutons on top of each bowl.

Make ahead tip: The recipe can be made ahead and kept chilled for 2 to 3 days before serving.

Alternatives: You can use any herb you like in place of the basil and substitute chicken broth for the V-8 or tomato juice; you would add 4 large peeled, seeded and chopped tomatoes if you choose to take out the juice. The soup can also be pureed if desired.

Vegetable, Chicken and Ginger Soup

Serves 8

Preparation time: 30 minutes

Cooking time: 15 minutes

Ingredients

9 cups chicken or vegetable stock

2 cups shredded Chinese cabbage

1 red pepper, julienne

1/4 pound shitake, cremini or domestic mushrooms, thinly sliced

4 scallions, thinly sliced

2-inch piece fresh ginger, julienne

1 boneless, skinless, chicken breast, cut into thin strips

6 oz. soba noodles, cooked, drained

2 Tablespoons rice wine vinegar

1/3 cup soy sauce

1/4 teaspoon red pepper flakes

1 bunch watercress, tough stems removed

3 Tablespoons whole cilantro leaves

Procedure

1. Bring the stock to a simmer in a soup pot. Add the cabbage, pepper, mushrooms, scallions and ginger and simmer 5 minutes.

2. Add the chicken and cook another 5 minutes. Stir in the noodles, rice vinegar, soy sauce and red pepper flakes and simmer 5 minutes more.

3. Right before serving add the watercress and cilantro. Serve immediately.

Make ahead tip: You can prepare the soup entirely through step 1 a day ahead or in the morning and complete step 2 right before serving.

Alternatives: You can use any other type of green leafy vegetable in place of the cabbage such as spinach, bok choy, escarole or Swiss chard. Tofu, shrimp or scallops can be used in place of the chicken. You can use flat leaf parsley in place of the cilantro or simply omit.

Spicy Thai Hot and Sour Soup with Shrimp

Serves 6

Preparation time: 15 minutes

Cooking time: 25 minutes

Ingredients

1 Tablespoon canola oil

2 cloves garlic, minced

2 shallots, minced

1 Tablespoon minced ginger

2 Thai chilies, seeded, minced

8 cups chicken or vegetable stock

3 Kaffir lime leaves, thinly sliced or 1 Tablespoon lime zest

1 stalk lemongrass, very thinly sliced

6 oz. shitake mushrooms, trimmed, thinly sliced

4 oz. rice vermicelli noodles, broken in half

1 1/2 pounds large shrimp, peeled, de-veined

6 Tablespoons fish sauce

6 Tablespoons lime juice

2 Tablespoons brown sugar

Whole cilantro leaves, garnish

Procedure

1. Heat the oil in a large saucepan and add the garlic, ginger, shallots and chilies. Cook over medium heat for 2 minutes. Add the lime leaves, lemongrass and shitakes and sauté another 4 minutes. Add the stock and bring to a boil. Reduce heat to medium-low and simmer for 10 minutes.

2. Meanwhile, soak the rice noodles in warm water for 5 minutes. Drain and rinse. Divide the noodles

into four large soup bowls.

3. Add the shrimp, fish sauce, lime juice and sugar to the soup and simmer until the shrimp is cooked through about 4 minutes. Ladle the soup over the noodles and garnish with cilantro leaves.

Make ahead tip: You can make this soup 2 days ahead and re-heat before serving. Add the cilantro leaves just before serving.

Alternatives: Either vegetable or fish stock can be used in place of the chicken broth. You can substitute scallops, boneless skinless chicken breasts, strips of beef or pork for the shrimp.

Seafood Chowder with Cilantro

Serves 8

Preparation time: 40 minutes

Cooking time: 35 minutes

Ingredients

7 cups vegetable or chicken stock

1 pound new potatoes, diced

4 cups frozen corn, defrosted

Salt, pepper

2 bay leaves

1 Tablespoon olive oil

1 large onion, diced

2 teaspoons thyme, chopped

4 cloves garlic, minced

2 celery stalks, diced

1 cup dry white wine

1 1/2 pounds mild white fish, haddock, snapper, cod or halibut, cut in chunks

1/4 cup chopped cilantro

Procedure

1. In a large saucepan combine 2 cups of the stock, half the potatoes, 2 cups of the corn, salt and pepper. Bring to a boil then reduce the heat and cover. Cook until potatoes are softened about 20 minutes. Puree the solids in a processor or with an immersion blender. Return to the saucepan, add 4 cups of the stock and the bay leaves and bring to a simmer over medium-low heat.

2. Meanwhile heat the oil in a large skillet and sauté the onion, thyme, garlic, celery, remaining potatoes and reserved 2 cups of corn until slightly browned, about 8 minutes. Season with salt and pepper. Add the wine and increase the heat to high, reduce the wine to about 1/4 cup.

3. Transfer the vegetables to the saucepan with the potato-corn puree, add the fish and cook through over low heat another 5 to 8 minutes.

4. Add the remaining 1 cup of stock if the soup is too thick. Season with salt and pepper and serve with cilantro on top.

Make ahead tip: The soup can be made ahead up to 3 days; simply add the fish right before serving. Remember to cook fish the day you buy it. The soup base can be frozen for up to 3 months without the fish.

Alternatives: You can use shrimp or scallops as well as, or in place of, the fish listed above. Flat leaf parsley can be used instead of cilantro if desired.

White Bean and Vegetable Soup with Pesto

Serves 6

Preparation time: 25 minutes

Cooking time: 40 minutes

Ingredients

2 cans cannelini beans, drained and rinsed

4 cups vegetable or chicken broth

2 Tablespoons olive oil

1 medium onion, chopped

4 garlic cloves, minced

2 carrots, diced

1 cup dry white wine

Salt, pepper to taste

1 28 oz. can tomatoes with juices, chopped

1/2 pound green beans, trimmed, cut into 1/2-inch diagonal slices

1 medium zucchini, diced

Pesto Sauce

2 cups loosely packed basil, washed, dried

3 cloves garlic, peeled

3 Tablespoons pine nuts, toasted

1/2 cup parmesan cheese

1/3 cup olive oil

Salt, pepper

▶

Procedure

1. Reserve 1/2 cup of the beans for later. Puree the rest of the beans in a processor with 1 cup of the vegetable broth.

2. Transfer the bean puree to a stockpot and stir in 2 cups of the broth. Heat the soup base over medium-high heat until simmering, season with salt and pepper. Cover and continue to simmer over low heat.

3. Meanwhile heat the oil in a large high sided saucepan over medium-heat and sauté the onion, garlic and carrots until slightly browned about 8 minutes. Add the wine and de-glaze the pan over high heat, scraping up all the brown bits in the bottom of the pan. Add salt and pepper, the remaining cup of broth, tomatoes, green beans and zucchini and cover, simmer another 10 minutes. Add to the stockpot with the white beans. Bring to a simmer and cook until all the vegetables are softened, about 5 to 10 minutes. Add the reserved whole beans and salt and pepper to taste.

4. For the pesto, combine the basil, garlic, pine nuts and cheese in a blender or processor and process until smooth. Add the oil gradually while the machine is running, season with salt and pepper to taste. If the pesto is too thick add a little water. Transfer to a serving bowl.

5. Heat the soup before serving and garnish with a dollop of the pesto.

   Make ahead tip: You can make the soup ahead and store it for 5 days in the refrigerator or freeze it for up to 3 months. The pesto will last for a week in the refrigerator or 3 months in the freezer.

   Alternatives: Chick peas, navy beans or white beans can be used in place of the cannellini beans.

Entrées

You can be very creative with an entrée. Many recipes have been born out of combinations invented with what is on hand. I would say the best way to cook is to make up your own dish with what is available to you in the market or in your own refrigerator, therefore; these recipes are ideas for you to try but feel free to incorporate your own personal style. If you like more garlic, add a clove or two, or if you have dark meat chicken in the freezer and would like to make the Chicken Souvlaki - try it with dark meat and you will have created your own dish.

Many of the following recipes can be made for guests and can be paired with a salad or side dish in a short amount of time. There are a couple recipes that take over an hour to cook so reserve these for a day when you can spend time in the kitchen and are not rushing around. This is why I always suggest you read through the recipe completely before preparing your meal. The last thing you want is to begin cooking and then find out the meat needs to marinate for 2 hours as in the Grilled Skirt Steak (page 82).

I am sure that these fabulous entrées will become part of your repertoire for everyday cooking as well as entertaining.

Recipes

Asian Chicken with Soy Sesame Glaze

Serves 4

Preparation time: 15 minutes

Marinating time: 30 minutes

Cooking time: 40 minutes

Ingredients

1 2 1/2 pounds chicken cut into eight pieces

3 scallions cut in 1/4-inch diagonal slices

5 cloves garlic, peeled, thinly sliced

1/4 cup dry sherry

2 Tablespoons rice wine vinegar

3 Tablespoons brown sugar

1/4 cup soy sauce

1/2 cup chicken broth

1 teaspoon toasted sesame oil

1 Tablespoon canola oil

1 Tablespoon sesame seeds, toasted, garnish

2 scallions, julienne, garnish

Procedure

1. Place the chicken in a large bowl and add the scallion, garlic, sherry, vinegar, sugar, soy, chicken broth and sesame oil. Marinate for 30 minutes at room temperature or 2 hours refrigerated.

2. Heat a large skillet over medium-high heat. Add the canola oil and sauté the chicken, reserving the marinade, until browned on all sides about 7 to 9 minutes. Add the marinade, cover, reduce the heat to low and simmer until the chicken is browned and cooked through about 15 minutes for the white meat. Remove the chicken breasts to a plate and cover loosely with foil. Continue to

cook the dark meat for another 8 minutes.

3. Uncover and remove the chicken to a serving dish. Increase the heat to high and reduce the sauce to a syrupy glaze, about 5 minutes.

4. Pour the glaze over the chicken and serve garnished with the sesame seeds and julienne scallions.

    Make ahead tip: The entire recipe can be made ahead up to two days ahead and re-heated right before serving.

    Alternatives: You can use all white meat for this recipe, for boneless, skinless chicken breast, sauté in step 2 and then cook with the sauce for 8 minutes before removing from the pan.

Braised Provencal Chicken with White Beans

Serves 4

Preparation time: 35 minutes

Marinating time: 30 minutes

Cooking time: 40 minutes

Ingredients

8 large chicken thighs

2 Tablespoons olive oil

Salt and pepper

1 Tablespoon minced rosemary

1 Tablespoon minced thyme

1 cup white wine

3 cloves garlic, thinly sliced

2 shallots, thinly sliced

6 plum tomatoes, diced

1/2 cup chicken stock

1 cup Kalamata olives, pitted, chopped

1 16 oz. can white beans, rinsed and drained

3 Tablespoons chopped basil, garnish

Procedure

1. Combine the chicken in a medium bowl with the oil, salt, pepper and herbs and set aside at room temperature for at least 30 minutes.

2. Heat a large skillet over medium high heat. Season chicken again with salt and pepper and brown it on all sides turning often about 10 minutes. Remove to a plate.

3. Pour off most of the drippings from the skillet and add the garlic and shallots and sauté about 2

minutes. Add the wine and increase the heat to high, deglaze the pan and reduce the wine to about 1/4 cup. Add the tomatoes and simmer 10 minutes. Season well with salt and pepper. Add the chicken stock and chicken, cover and simmer until chicken is cooked through, about 15 minutes. Stir in the olives and beans and heat briefly. Taste for seasoning.

4. Transfer the chicken to a large serving platter and garnish with the basil.

Make ahead tip: You can make the entire recipe up to two days ahead and re-heat for 10 minutes from room temperature before serving.

Alternatives: Boneless, skinless chicken breast can be used in place of the dark meat. In step 2 sear the breast 3 minutes on each side and then add back to the pan in step 3 for 6 minutes then serve.

Chicken Souvlaki

Serves 4

Preparation time: 1 hour 30 minutes

Marinating time: 1 hour or overnight

Cooking time: 8 minutes

Ingredients

3 Tablespoons extra-virgin olive oil

3 Tablespoons dry white wine

2 Tablespoons lemon juice

1/4 cup minced onion

1 garlic clove, minced

1 teaspoon dried oregano

Salt and freshly ground pepper, to taste

1 1/2 pounds boneless, skinless chicken, cut into 1-inch pieces

Lemon wedges for garnish

Flat-leaf parsley leaves for garnish

Yogurt Sauce:

2 cups plain whole milk yogurt

½ English cucumber, peeled, halved, seeded and grated

Salt to taste

3 garlic cloves, minced

1 Tablespoon chopped mint

1 Tablespoon chopped dill

2 Tablespoons olive oil

1 Tablespoon lemon juice

Procedure

1. In a bowl, stir together the olive oil, wine, lemon juice, onion, garlic, oregano, salt and pepper. Add the chicken pieces and turn to coat evenly. Cover and refrigerate for one to two hours.

2. If using bamboo skewers, put four skewers in cold water to cover for thirty minutes before using.

3. Meanwhile drain the yogurt in a cheesecloth lined sieve over a bowl for about an hour. Discard the water and transfer the yogurt to a medium bowl.

4. Transfer the grated cucumber to a sieve, toss with salt and drain over a bowl for about 20 minutes.

5. Add the cucumber to the yogurt with the garlic, mint, dill, olive oil, lemon juice and salt to taste. Mix well and taste for seasoning. Serve chilled.

6. Heat a grill pan over medium high heat. Remove the chicken pieces from the marinade and drain the bamboo skewers, if using. Thread the chicken pieces onto the bamboo or stainless-steel skewers, dividing the pieces evenly among them. Place the skewers on the grill turning once, until the chicken is opaque throughout, 3 to 4 minutes per side. Season with salt and pepper to taste.

7. Transfer to a serving platter and garnish with lemon wedges and parsley. Serve immediately with the yogurt sauce.

Make ahead tip: You can make the skewers with dark meat chicken the day before and marinate overnight. They can be frozen in the marinade for up to 3 months. Defrost in the refrigerator overnight before cooking. The yogurt sauce can be made three days ahead and kept refrigerated.

Alternatives: Lamb, dark meat chicken or beef can be used in place of the chicken breast. Ask for leg of lamb or beef used for stew. Be sure to marinate overnight for these cuts of meat.

Italian Chicken with Prosciutto and Basil

Serves 4

Preparation time: 20 minutes

Cooking time: 25 minutes

Ingredients

1 Tablespoon butter

2 Tablespoon olive oil

3 medium shallots, minced

3 large garlic cloves, minced

Salt and pepper

4 large chicken breast halves on the bone, with the skin on

4 thin slices prosciutto, cut in half

12 large basil leaves, plus 2 Tablespoons chopped basil

1/2 cup dry white wine

1/3 cup chicken stock

2 Tablespoons Dijon mustard

1/3 cup heavy cream

Procedure

1. Preheat the oven to 350.
2. Melt the butter and 1 tablespoon of the olive oil in a small skillet. Add half the shallots and half the garlic and sauté 3 minutes. Season with salt and pepper and transfer to a small bowl.
3. Loosen the skin from the chicken breasts being careful not to tear the skin and spread the shallot mixture evenly between the four halves. Top each half with a piece of prosciutto and 3 basil leaves. Smooth the skin over the basil and season well with salt and pepper.
4. Heat a large skillet over medium-high heat and add the second tablespoon of olive oil and sauté

the chicken skin side down for 3 to 4 minutes, turn over and sauté on the other side for another 3 to 4 minutes. Set the chicken in a baking sheet and roast skin side up for 15 to 18 minutes until cooked through. Transfer the chicken to a plate and keep warm.

5. Meanwhile, add the remaining chopped shallots and garlic to the skillet and sauté 2 minutes. Over medium heat. Add the wine increase the heat to high and deglaze the pan, add the chicken stock and heavy cream, cook until slightly thickened about 4 minutes. Add any reserved drippings from the baking sheet, the chopped basil and season with salt and pepper.

6. Cut the breasts in half right through the skin and bone and set onto a serving plate. Spoon the sauce over the chicken and serve.

Make ahead tip: You can make the recipe a day before up until the chicken is roasted in the oven and then roast it right before serving. Or the whole recipe can be made ahead and re-heated in the oven for 5 minutes before serving at 350. Re-heat the sauce separately in a small saucepan and then spoon over the chicken.

Alternatives: If you would like to use boneless skinless chicken breast you would proceed with the recipe and bake it for 8 minutes in step number 4. The cream can be omitted from the sauce if desired, simply add more chicken stock and reduce slightly to thicken.

Sweet and Spicy Sticky Chicken

Serves 4

Preparation time: 15 minutes

Cooking time: 30 minutes

Ingredients

2/3 cup sugar

2 Tablespoons lime juice

1/2 cup soy sauce

1 Tablespoon minced ginger

2 cloves garlic, minced

2 teaspoons red pepper flakes

1 1/2 Tablespoons canola oil

2 pounds boneless, chicken thighs or breasts

Salad:

2 carrots, peeled, julienne

1/2 pound daikon radish, peeled, julienne

1/2 cup rice vinegar

1/4 cup sugar

1 teaspoon salt

Cilantro sprigs, garnish

Procedure

1. Whisk together the sugar, lime juice, soy, ginger, garlic and chili flakes in a large bowl. Set aside.

2. Heat a skillet over high heat and add the oil, sear the chicken skin side down until golden brown on each side about 8 minutes. Remove to a plate and set aside. Discard the oil.

3. Add the sauce to the pan and bring to a boil. Simmer until slightly thickened about 5 minutes. Return the chicken to the pan skin side up, cover and cook until cooked through 15 minutes for dark meat and 8 minutes for breasts. Turn the chicken once or twice while cooking. Remove the chicken to a platter and cover with foil. Reduce the sauce until very syrupy and then pour over the chicken.

4. Meanwhile, combine the carrots and daikon radish in a medium bowl, add the vinegar, sugar and salt and toss well. Chill for 20 minutes.

5. Surround the chicken with the salad and garnish with cilantro sprigs.

Make ahead tip: The recipe can be made a day ahead and re-heated or made in the morning and re-heated before serving for 10 minutes in a 350 oven. The salad can be made a day ahead as well.

Alternatives: You can use julienne red and yellow pepper in place of the carrots and add watercress to the salad for more color if desired.

Grilled Turkey Burgers with Caramelized Onion Relish

Serves 4

Preparation time: 15 minutes

Cooking time: 45 minutes

Ingredients

2 large onions, sliced very thinly

1 Tablespoon olive oil

1 Tablespoon Dijon mustard

2 Tablespoons balsamic vinegar

2 Tablespoons dark brown sugar

Salt and pepper, to taste

1 pound lean ground turkey

2 eggs

1/2 cup bread crumbs

2 small shallots, minced

2 Tablespoons chopped flat leaf parsley

Procedure

1. Heat a large skillet for a three minutes over medium heat. Add onions and oil and sauté until translucent. Lower heat and cook stirring once or twice until caramelized about 30 minutes. Add mustard, vinegar, sugar and 1/3 cup water, season to taste with salt and pepper. Cover and cook another 4 minutes. Uncover and simmer until liquid is evaporated about 3 minutes. Set aside.

2. Combine the ground turkey, eggs, breadcrumbs, shallots, parsley, salt and pepper in a large bowl and mix well. Shape into four patties.

3. Heat the grill for 5 minutes over high heat. Grill the burgers until firm to the touch about 5 to 7 minutes on each side. Serve with the onion relish.

Make ahead tip: You can make the onions and keep them refrigerated for up to 5 days. The patties can be formed the day before or made ahead and frozen for up to 3 months.

Alternatives: You can use ground beef, buffalo or chicken in place of the lean ground turkey. Cook the same amount of time.

Beef Medallions with Caramelized Onions and Arugula

Serves 4

Preparation time: 40 minutes

Cooking time: 45 minutes

Ingredients

1 1/4 pounds beef tenderloin, trimmed of all fat

2 Tablespoons olive oil

2 large onions, thinly sliced

4 plum tomatoes, roughly chopped

2 bunches arugula, washed, drained, roughly chopped

Salt, pepper

1 Tablespoon butter

2 shallots, minced

1 cup brandy

1/2 cup beef or veal stock

2 Tablespoons chopped flat leaf parsley

Procedure

1. Heat the oven to 400. Cut the beef into four even slices.

2. Heat 1 tablespoon of the olive oil in a large skillet. Sauté the onions over medium heat 5 minutes, season with salt and pepper. Lower heat and cook 30 minutes, until caramel colored, stirring once or twice. Stir in tomatoes and arugula and cook until arugula is wilted, set aside.

3. Heat a medium skillet and add the remaining tablespoon olive oil over medium-high heat. Sear the meat until browned about 3 to 4 minutes per side seasoning with salt and pepper as you go. Transfer to a baking sheet.

4. Place the beef in the oven for 5 to 10 minutes depending on desired doneness.

5. Add the butter to the same skillet and sauté the shallots over medium high heat until translucent about 2 minutes. Season with salt and pepper. Add the brandy increase the heat to high and reduce to a few tablespoons. Add the stock and bring to a boil. Reduce by half and then taste for seasoning. Remove from heat.

6. Mound a serving plate with the onion-arugula mixture. Place the meat on top. Ladle the sauce over the meat and garnish with chopped parsley.

Make Ahead Tip: The entire recipe can be made a day ahead up to step 4. Make the sauce and warm up in a skillet before serving while you are finishing the beef in the oven.

Alternatives: You can use pork tenderloin or lamb chops in place of the beef. Spinach, Swiss chard or bok choy can be substituted for the arugula.

Grilled Skirt Steak with the Best Marinade

Serves 4

Preparation time: 15 minutes

Marinating time: 2 hours

Cooking time: 20 minutes

Ingredients

1 1/2 pounds skirt, flank or hanger steak, scored

3 shallots, minced

1/4 cup balsamic vinegar

1/4 cup soy sauce

4 cloves garlic, minced

1/4 cup olive oil

1 Tablespoon Dijon mustard

1 Tablespoon rosemary, chopped

Fresh black pepper

1 cup dry red wine

2 scallions, julienne, garnish

Procedure

1. Place the steak in a shallow baking dish.
2. Combine marinade ingredients up to wine and scallions in a medium bowl. Pour over steak and marinate about 2 hours or overnight, refrigerated.
3. Half hour before grilling remove the steak from the refrigerator.
4. Heat grill pan for about 5 minutes. Grill steak, reserving marinade, 7 to 8 minutes on each side for medium-rare meat. Remove to a cutting board.

5. Bring marinade to a boil with the red wine in a small saucepan, boil for 3 to 4 minutes. Set aside. Slice meat thinly against the grain. Place on a serving platter and pour the marinade over. Garnish with the scallions and serve.

Make ahead tip: The steak can be marinated overnight or frozen in the marinade for up to 3 months.

Alternatives: Any cut of meat can be used such as London broil, tri-tip, pork tenderloin, lamb chops or lamb loin.

Tuscan Meat Loaf Braised in White Wine

Serves 6

Preparation time: 35 minutes

Cooking time: 1 hour 15 minutes

Ingredients

1 oz. dried wild mushrooms

1 pound ground beef

1/4 pound ground turkey

1/4 pound ground pork

1 cup bread crumbs

1/3 cup grated parmesan

2 large eggs

1/2 teaspoon salt

Fresh pepper, to taste

2 Tablespoons olive oil

1 medium onion, finely diced

2 oz. finely chopped prosciutto

2 teaspoons chopped rosemary

1 Tablespoon chopped thyme

3 cloves garlic, minced

2 cups dry white wine

3 Tablespoons tomato paste

Procedure

1. Heat the oven to 375. Combine the dried mushrooms in a small bowl with 1 cup of boiling water.

2. Place the meat in a medium bowl and add the bread crumbs, cheese, eggs, salt and pepper and mix well.

3. Meanwhile, drain the mushrooms, reserving the liquid. Strain the liquid and save. Chop the mushrooms and set aside.

4. Heat the olive oil in a large skillet and sauté the onion for 3 minutes over medium heat. Add the prosciutto, rosemary, thyme and garlic and sauté 2 minutes. Add the reserved mushroom liquid to the skillet and cook over high heat 2 minutes. Allow to cool slightly. Add to the meat mixture and mix well. Form the meat into two loaves with your hands. Transfer the loaves to an oblong baking pan.

5. Combine the wine, tomato paste and reserved porcini mushrooms in a medium bowl and mix well. Pour around the meat loaf and cover loosely with foil.

6. Bake for about 1 hour 15 minutes, basting occasionally with the juices. Remove the loaf to a cutting board and allow to rest for 15 minutes. Slice the meat loaf and pour the sauce over.

Make ahead tip: The meat loaf can be made a day ahead and cooked before serving or cooked completely and then re-heated before serving in a 325 oven for 20 minutes.

Alternatives: You can use all ground turkey or chicken in place of the beef and pork if desired. You would reduce the cooking time to 40 minutes. Omit the proscuitto or substitute pancetta is desired.

Spice-Crusted Lamb Chops with Balsamic Glaze

Serves 6

Preparation time: 10 minutes

Cooking time: 20 minutes

Ingredients

2 Tablespoons coriander seeds

2 Tablespoons cumin seeds

2 Tablespoons fennel seeds

1 1/2 teaspoons salt

1/2 teaspoon fresh pepper

12 1 1/4 inch thick lamb loin chops

2 Tablespoons canola oil

1 cup balsamic vinegar

1/3 cup red wine, Cabernet or Merlot are suggested

Procedure

1. Combine the seeds, salt and pepper in a spice grinder and grind to a sandy texture, not a powder. Transfer to a baking sheet.

2. Rinse the lamb chops lightly and pat dry. Coat the chops in the spice mixture, pressing the spices on to the meat.

3. Heat the oven to 350. Heat a large skillet over medium-high heat. Add one tablespoon of the oil. Lower the heat to medium and add half the chops Cook about 3 to 4 minutes per side, until the crust is browned and then transfer to a baking sheet. Add the remaining oil and sauté the remaining chops. Add to the baking sheet and cook in the oven for 5 minutes until springy to the touch for medium rare chops.

4. Meanwhile bring the vinegar and wine to a boil in a small saucepan over medium-high heat. Lower the heat to medium and simmer the sauce for about 5 to 8 minutes until it is thick and syrupy.

5. Remove the chops from the oven and divide them between four dinner plates, drizzle with the balsamic syrup and serve.

Make ahead tip: You can cook the lamb 4 minutes per side a day head and refrigerate on the baking sheet. Remove the chops half an hour before cooking and finish in the oven for the last 5 minutes. The sauce can be made entirely ahead and re-heated before serving.

Alternatives: Pork or beef tenderloin can be used in place of the lamb.

Provencal Lamb Stew

Serves 6

Preparation time: 30 minutes

Cooking time: 1 hour 30 minutes

Ingredients

2 1/2 pounds of lamb shoulder, trimmed, cubed

1/4 cup flour

Salt and pepper

3 Tablespoons canola oil

3 cups beef stock

1 cup red wine

1 Tablespoon tomato paste

3 garlic cloves, minced

1 bay leaf

4 sprigs fresh thyme

2 sprigs rosemary

Salt, pepper

4 large carrots, peeled, large dice

1 large onion, chopped

8 small new potatoes, quartered

1/3 cup flat leaf parsley, chopped

Procedure

1. In a medium bowl combine the flour, lamb, salt and pepper and toss to coat the lamb.

2. In a large high sided saucepan heat 2 tablespoons of the oil over medium-high heat. Add the lamb and brown all over about 5 to 8 minutes.

3. Add the stock, wine, tomato paste, garlic and herbs and bring to a boil, reduce heat, cover and simmer for 30 minutes.

4. Meanwhile, heat the remaining tablespoon of oil in a large high sided skillet and add the onions and carrots. Sauté them shaking the pan occasionally for about 8 minutes. Add the potatoes and sauté until slightly browned seasoning with salt and pepper another 8 to 10 minutes.

5. Add the vegetables to the lamb. Bring to a simmer and cook until lamb is tender about 1 to 1/2 hours. Season with salt and pepper and turn off the heat. Allow the stew to sit covered for about 15 minutes before serving.

6. Remove the sprigs of herbs and the bay leaf, serve garnished with the chopped parsley.

Make ahead tip: You can make the stew up to 3 days ahead and re-heat it when you are ready or freeze the stew for up to 3 months.

Alternatives: Beef can be used in place of the lamb and other vegetables such as mushrooms, shallots, peas or pearl onions can be added to the stew.

Seared Tuna Burgers with Wasabi Mayonnaise

Serves 4

Preparation time: 15 minutes

Cooking time: 4 minutes

Ingredients

1 1/2 pounds tuna fillet, finely chopped in the processor

Freshly ground pepper

1 minced shallot

2 Tablespoons soy sauce or Tamari

1/2 cup mayonnaise

2 teaspoons wasabi powder mixed with 1 Tablespoon of water

2 Tablespoons chopped cilantro

Salt to taste

1 Tablespoon canola oil

Procedure

1. Combine the tuna with the pepper, shallot and soy sauce in a medium bowl. Shape into four equal patties.

2. In a small bowl combine the mayonnaise, wasabi powder paste and cilantro. Add the salt and pepper to taste. Chill.

3. Heat a large skillet over medium-high heat and add the canola oil. Add the tuna burgers and sear until the outside is browned and crispy about 2 minutes on each side. Remove the tuna burgers to a plate.

4. Spoon a dollop of the mayonnaise on top of each and serve.

Make ahead tip: The burgers can be formed a few hours ahead and cooked at the last minute. The sauce will last up to 5 days in the refrigerator.

Alternatives: Salmon can be used in place of the tuna, sauté for 5 minutes per side. Chicken or turkey breast can also be substituted simply sauté for 6 to 8 minutes per side until cooked through.

Sesame Coated Salmon with Indonesian Soy Sauce

Serves 4

Preparation time: 20 minutes

Cooking time: 15 minutes

Ingredients

2 Tablespoons ketchup

2 Tablespoons ketjap manis*

2 Tablespoons red wine vinegar

1 Tablespoon light brown sugar or honey

1 teaspoon curry powder

1/2 teaspoon ground cumin

1/2 teaspoon Tabasco

1/2 teaspoon salt

1/4 cup cilantro leaves, chopped

1/4 to 1/2 cup water

1/2 cup flour seasoned with salt and pepper

3 egg whites

3/4 cup black and white sesame seeds, lightly toasted

4, 6 oz. salmon, fillets, skinned

Canola oil

Cilantro leaves, garnish

Procedure

1. In a small saucepan combine the ketchup, ketjap manis, vinegar, sugar, curry, cumin, Tabasco, salt and cilantro, whisk adding enough water until it is the consistency of a thick sauce. Bring   to a simmer over medium-low heat for 5 minutes. Set aside.

2. Place the seasoned flour on a baking sheet. Place the egg whites in a medium bowl and lightly whisk. Place the sesame seeds on a baking sheet.

3. Dip the salmon in the flour, egg whites, and then in the sesame seeds and turn to coat.

4. Heat a large skillet over medium high heat and add a little canola oil. Sauté the salmon until slightly golden and crisp about 3 minutes per side. Transfer to a baking sheet and finish cooking in the oven until medium-rare about 7 minutes.

5. Re-heat the sauce until bubbling. Transfer the salmon to dinner plates and spoon some sauce over the fish and garnish with cilantro. Pass any remaining sauce.

Make ahead tip: The entire recipe can be made a day ahead up to step 5. Omit baking the salmon until right before serving.

Alternatives: You can use tuna in place of the salmon. After dipping in the seeds, sear the tuna for 3 minutes per side and omit baking in the oven.

*Ketjap Manis can be found in gourmet stores in the Asian sauce section.

Sautéed Tilapia with Asparagus and Gingered Tomatoes

Serves 4

Preparation time: 20 minutes

Cooking time: 30 minutes

Ingredients

2 Tablespoons olive oil

2 large onions, halved, thinly sliced

1 Tablespoon Madras curry powder

1 pint cherry tomatoes

1 Tablespoon minced ginger

2 garlic cloves, minced

1 pound asparagus cut into diagonal slices, blanched

1 1/2 pounds tilapia fillets, skin removed

Flour for dredging

Salt and pepper, to taste

Canola oil for sautéing

1 lemon cut into wedges, garnish

Procedure

1. Heat a large skillet over medium-high heat for a few minutes add 1 tablespoon of the oil and sauté the onions until translucent, about 4 minutes. Lower the heat to medium-low and cook the onions until caramelized, about 30 minutes stirring once or twice. Add the curry and salt and pepper to taste. Transfer to a small bowl and cover with foil to keep warm.

2. Heat the remaining tablespoon of olive oil in the same skillet over medium-high heat and sauté the tomatoes with the ginger and garlic for 3 minutes. Season with salt and pepper. Add the asparagus and cook 2 minutes. Cover and set aside.

3. Dip the fish in flour seasoned with salt and pepper, shaking off any excess.

4. Heat a large skillet over high heat and add a thin layer of canola oil. Sauté the fish until firm to the touch, 4 minutes per side.

5. Divide the fish between four dinner plates. Top with the curried onions and spoon the vegetables around the edges. Garnish each plate with a wedge of lemon and serve.

Make ahead tip: The entire recipe can be made ahead up to cooking the fish which could be done right before serving.

Alternatives: You can use other mild white fish such as snapper, sea bass, halibut, sole or flounder. Any green vegetable can be substituted for the asparagus such as broccoli, green beans, snow peas or snap peas.

Pork with Honey-Balsamic Glaze

Serves 6

Preparation time: 10 minutes

Cooking time: 25 minutes

Ingredients

1/2 cup balsamic vinegar

3 Tablespoons honey

1 Tablespoon olive oil

1 Tablespoon chopped rosemary

4 cloves garlic, minced

1 Tablespoon Dijon mustard

Salt and pepper, to taste

1 package pork tenderloin, about 2 pounds

1 Tablespoon canola oil

Rosemary branches, garnish

Procedure

1. Combine the vinegar, honey, olive oil, rosemary, garlic, mustard, salt and pepper in a small bowl and whisk, set aside.

2. Heat the oven to 350.

3. Heat a medium skillet over medium-high heat. Add the canola oil and add the pork. Brown on each side seasoning with salt and pepper, about 3 to 4 minutes.

4. Transfer the pork to a shallow baking dish and pour the balsamic glaze over. Roast the pork in the oven for 20 minutes basting once or twice until the internal temperature reaches 145. Remove from the oven and allow the pork to rest 5 minutes before slicing.

5. Slice the pork and pour the sauce over, garnish with the rosemary branches.

Make ahead tip: You can make this recipe ahead up to a day before and roast before serving.

Alternatives: You can use any other meat such as beef tenderloin, chicken breast, lamb chops or lamb loin.

Pork Tenderloin with Soy-Ginger Glaze

Serves 6

Preparation time: 15 minutes

Marinating time: 30 minutes

Cooking time: 30 minutes

Ingredients

2 Tablespoons canola oil

2 1-pound pork tenderloins, trimmed, silver skin removed

1/3 cup soy sauce

5 Tablespoons apricot preserves

4 garlic cloves, peeled

2 Tablespoons roughly chopped ginger

3 Tablespoons honey

Fresh pepper, to taste

1/4 cup cilantro leaves or flat leaf parsley

Steamed Jasmine rice

Procedure

1. Heat a large skillet and add a tablespoon of the canola oil. Sear the pork all over seasoning with salt and pepper, about 6 minutes. Remove to a baking dish. Combine the soy, preserves, garlic, remaining oil, honey, pepper and cilantro in a processor and process. Pour over the pork and turn to coat. Marinate at least 30 minutes or overnight in the refrigerator.

2. Heat the oven to 375. Roast the pork basting occasionally until medium rare about 25 minutes. When a thermometer is inserted into the meat it should read 145 degrees. Remove from the oven and allow to rest before carving.

3. Add a little hot water to the baking dish and scrape up the marinade into a sauce, drizzle over the pork and serve with rice if desired.

Make ahead tip: The recipe can be made ahead up to a day before through step 1 and then roasted before serving.

Alternatives: Beef tenderloin, lamb chops or boneless, skinless chicken breast or thighs can be used in place of the pork.

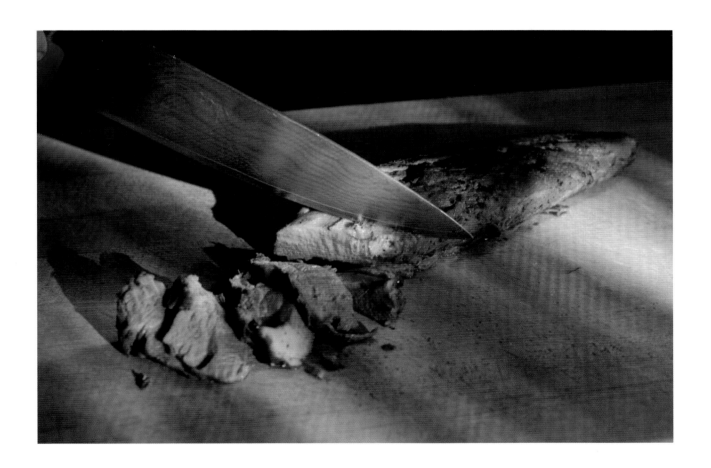

Side Dishes

When you are preparing a meal it is always good to start with the entrée and then work back from there to decide what you want to serve with it. Side dishes can be as creative as the main course and I am a big fan of mixing textures and colors to enhance the presentation of the plate.

Vegetables are a central theme as more and more people are adding a variety of vegetables to their diet. I think it is important to eat foods that are in season and to seek out local produce that has been grown organically. I recommend the farmer's markets that are popping up everywhere for local produce. Grains and legumes are also a wonderful addition to your meal as they are satisfying as well as nutritious. I often make a complete meal out of side dishes for lunch and find this way of eating gives me a boost of energy that often is missing with animal protein.

I love side dishes as they are versatile and can be eaten at room temperature or cold as a salad. I often put together two or three side dishes and enjoy this as a small meal. Try mixing different sides with your entree and see what works for you.

Recipes

Roasted Beets with Shallots and Rosemary

Serves 4

Preparation time: 10 minutes

Cooking time: 40 minutes

Ingredients

1 1/2 pounds beets, washed, quartered

2 shallots, halved, thinly sliced

3 Tablespoons lemon juice

1/4 cup extra virgin olive oil

Salt, pepper, to taste

2 Tablespoons minced rosemary or mint

Procedure

1. Heat the oven to 400. Place the beets on a baking sheet. Toss with olive oil, salt and roast until tender, about 40 minutes.
2. Meanwhile, combine remaining ingredients in a medium bowl.
3. Allow beets to cool enough to handle and slice into julienne strips or small dice.
4. Toss with vinaigrette and serve warm or room temperature.

Make ahead tip: You can prepare the salad up to 3 days ahead.

Alternatives: Use scallions in place of the shallots and orange or lime juice in place of the lemon if desired.

Curried Lentil Salad with Walnuts

Serves 4

Preparation time: 20 minutes

Cooking time: 20 minutes

Ingredients

1 cup French lentils

1 medium carrot, diced

1 onion, diced

1 bay leaf

1 red pepper, diced

4 scallions, thinly sliced

1/2 cup walnuts, roughly chopped

1/3 cup chopped mint

2 cloves garlic, minced

6 Tablespoons lemon juice

2 teaspoons curry powder

Salt, pepper

1/4 cup olive oil

Procedure

1. Combine the lentils, carrot, onion and bay leaf in a medium saucepan with cold water to cover by 2 inches. Bring to a simmer and cover, simmer about 20 minutes, until tender. Drain. Transfer to a medium bowl and remove bay leaf. Add the red pepper, scallions, walnuts and mint.
2. Combine the garlic, lemon and curry in a small bowl and whisk. Add salt and pepper to taste. Add the olive oil slowly and taste for seasoning. Toss the dressing with the lentils.
3. Serve at room temperature.

Make ahead tip: The salad can be prepared up to 3 days ahead.

Alternatives: Other beans can be used such as canned chick peas, black beans or white beans. Almonds, pine nuts or hazelnuts can be used in place of the walnuts.

Roasted Curried Cauliflower

Serves 6

Preparation time: 15 minutes

Cooking time: 35 minutes

Ingredients

1 large cauliflower

1 large onion, cut in large chunks

1 teaspoon cumin seeds

1/4 cup olive oil

1 Tablespoon curry powder

1 teaspoon salt

2 Tablespoons chopped cilantro

Procedure

1. Heat the oven to 400.
2. Break up the cauliflower into medium pieces and combine with the onions on a roasting pan.
3. Toast the cumin seeds until fragrant in a small skillet, about 5 minutes.
4. Combine the seeds, olive oil, curry and salt in a medium bowl and whisk. Toss the sauce with the vegetables.
5. Roast for 35 minutes. Serve garnished with the cilantro.

Make ahead tip: The cauliflower can be roasted a day ahead and then re-heated before serving in a 350 oven for 10 minutes, uncovered.

Alternatives: Brussels sprouts, zucchini, mushrooms, eggplant and red or yellow peppers can be used or included in the above recipe. Parsley can be used in place of the cilantro as well as other spices such as fennel, mustard seeds or saffron. If you don't like the spices simply roast it plain with olive oil, salt and pepper.

Brown and Wild Rice Salad

Serves 4

Preparation time: 15 minutes

Cooking time: 40 minutes

Ingredients

1 pound red onions cut into 1/2-inch chunks

2 Tablespoons olive oil

1 cup wild rice

1 cup brown rice

1/2 cup wheat berries

1 red pepper, diced

1/2 cup currants, raisins or dried cranberries (optional)

4 scallions, thinly sliced

3 Tablespoons soy sauce

3 teaspoons thyme, chopped

1/2 cup flat leaf parsley, chopped

Procedure

1. Heat the oven to 400. Combine the onions and olive oil in a shallow baking dish and roast about 30 minutes.

2. Meanwhile cook the wild rice in 3 cups water in a small saucepan, covered until tender about 40 minutes.

3. Combine the brown rice and wheat berries in another small saucepan and cover with 3 1/2 cups water, cover, simmer until rice is tender about 25 to 30 minutes.

4. Drain rice, if necessary, and transfer to a bowl to cool slightly.

5. Add remaining ingredients and toss well. Taste for seasoning and serve room temperature.

Make ahead tip: The entire recipe can be made up to 5 days ahead and served cold or room temperature.

Alternatives: You can omit the wheat berries or use all brown or wild rice if desired. Canned beans such as chick peas or black beans can be added for a complete protein. Simply rinse and drain them and toss them in at the end.

Grilled Corn and Roasted Red Pepper Salad

Serves 6

Preparation time: 15 minutes

Cooking time: 20 minutes

Ingredients

5 large ears corn, husked

3 red peppers

3 scallions, thinly sliced

10 basil leaves, chopped

2 garlic cloves, minced

3 Tablespoons lemon juice

1/3 cup olive oil

Salt, pepper

Basil leaves whole, garnish

Procedure

1. Heat the grill. Grill corn all over for about 15-20 minutes. Remove to a cutting board and allow to cool.
2. Roast the peppers on top of a gas flame or under the broiler. Peppers should be completely blackened. Remove peppers to a bowl and cover for 15 to 20 minutes.
3. Stand corn on its end and shave off the kernels. Place in a serving bowl. Remove skin, seeds and membrane from the peppers and dice, add to the bowl.
4. Combine the scallions, basil, garlic, lemon and olive oil in a small bowl and whisk, season with salt and pepper to taste and pour over salad. Toss well and taste, adjust seasoning.

Make ahead tip: The salad can be prepared ahead up to 4 days.

Alternatives: If it is tomato season, add 1 pint cherry tomatoes, rinsed and halved to the above salad. You can omit the roasted peppers and serve the salad as is or use chopped or cherry tomatoes instead. Black beans can also be added for a variation.

Seamed Spinach with Spicy Ginger Dressing

Serves 6

Preparation time: 15 minutes

Cooking time: 5 minutes

Ingredients

2 Tablespoons canola oil

1 Tablespoon finely minced ginger

3 cloves minced garlic

3 Tablespoons soy sauce

2 Tablespoons rice vinegar

2 teaspoons sugar

1 Tablespoon toasted sesame oil

1 teaspoon red pepper flakes

2 pounds baby spinach, tough stems removed

2 Tablespoons toasted sesame seeds, garnish

Procedure

1. In a small skillet over medium high heat sauté the ginger and garlic in the canola oil for 30 seconds. Transfer to a serving bowl and add the soy sauce, rice vinegar, sugar, sesame oil and red pepper flakes.

2. Place spinach in a large saucepan with a small amount of water in the bottom. Cover and steam until wilted about 3 to 5 minutes. Transfer to a colander and drain well pressing down on the greens to remove the excess water.

4. Transfer the spinach to the bowl toss with the dressing and serve sprinkled with toasted sesame seeds as a garnish.

Make ahead tip: The entire recipe can be made up to 3 days ahead and served cold or room temperature.

Alternatives: Any green leafy vegetable can be used such as bok choy, Swiss chard, escarole or kale.

Caponata

Serves 6

Preparation time: 20 minutes

Cooking time: 25 minutes

Ingredients

1 medium eggplant, cut into small dice

3 Tablespoons olive oil

2 stalks celery, finely diced

1 small onion, chopped finely

4 cloves garlic, minced

1/3 cup red wine vinegar

1 Tablespoon sugar

1, 20 oz. can plum tomatoes, with juices, chopped

2 Tablespoons capers, rinsed

1/2 cup Kalamata olives, pitted, chopped

Salt, pepper

3 Tablespoons flat leaf parsley, chopped

Parmesan cheese, shaved.

Procedure

1. Heat a large saucepan and add 2 tablespoons of the olive oil. Sauté the eggplant in batches until golden, remove to drain on a paper towel lined tray.

2. Add the remaining oil and sauté the celery and onions for 5 minutes. Add garlic, vinegar, sugar and tomatoes and simmer for 10 minutes over low heat. Add the capers, olives, salt, pepper and eggplant. Simmer for 15 minutes. Taste and adjust seasoning.

3. Serve the caponata warm, garnished with the shaved parmesan.

Make ahead tip: The entire recipe can be made up to 3 days ahead and served at room temperature or re-heated. It can be frozen for up to 3 months.

Alternatives: For an appetizer serve the caponata on toasted rounds of baguette with shaved parmesan or chevre on top.

Serves 6

Preparation time: 15 minutes

Cooking time: 17 minutes

Ingredients

1 Tablespoon olive oil

2 medium shallots, minced

3 cloves garlic, minced

1/4 to 1/2 teaspoon red pepper flakes

4 oz. pancetta diced

1 medium head escarole, washed, chopped

1 Tablespoon chopped rosemary

2 teaspoons chopped thyme

Salt, pepper

2 cans white beans, rinsed and drained

1/2 cup chicken broth

3 Tablespoons chopped flat leaf parsley, garnish

¾ cup grated Pecorino cheese

Procedure

1. Heat the oil in a large high-sided skillet over medium-high heat and sauté the shallots, garlic, red pepper flakes and pancetta about 3 minutes.

2. Add the escarole, rosemary, thyme and salt and pepper to taste. Sauté until wilted about 2 minutes over medium heat. Add the beans and broth and bring to a simmer for about 10 minutes.

3. Season to taste with salt and pepper and serve with the parsley and cheese on top.

Make ahead tip: The entire recipe can be made 3 days ahead and served room temperature or re-heated in a medium saucepan before serving.

Alternatives: Any other bean can be used in place of the white beans. Sausages or pancetta can be substituted for the pancetta in step 1. Shaved or grated parmesan is a great topping instead of the pecorino along with or instead of the chopped parsley.

Tabouli Salad with Parsley and Mint

Serves 4 to 6

Preparation time: 20 minutes

Cooking time: 15 minutes

Ingredients

1 cup bulgur wheat, medium grain

3/4 cup boiling water

2 cups flat leaf parsley, finely chopped

4 plum tomatoes finely chopped

3 scallions, minced

1/2 cup mint leaves, chopped

1 cucumber, peeled, seeded, finely diced

3 Tablespoons olive oil

1/2 cup lemon juice

Salt, pepper

Procedure

1. Combine the bulgur and water in a small bowl and cover; let sit for 15 minutes. Uncover, season with a pinch of salt and transfer to a large bowl.

2. Add the remaining ingredients and toss well. Taste for seasoning.

Make ahead tip: You can make the salad up to 2 days ahead. Or you can make it 5 days ahead and add the chopped tomatoes and herbs the day you serve it. Chop them both a few hours before serving to preserve their color and texture.

Alternatives: Cooked short grain brown rice can be used in place of the bulgur wheat for a brown rice salad.

Couscous with Lentils and Feta

Serves 6

Preparation time: 10 minutes

Cooking time: 7 minutes

Ingredients

10 oz. instant couscous

2 1/2 cups chicken or vegetable broth

1 teaspoon salt

1/2 teaspoon turmeric

1/2 teaspoon ground cumin

1/2 teaspoon black pepper

2 plum tomatoes, chopped

1/2 cup French lentils, cooked until tender

4 Tablespoons chopped flat leaf parsley or mint

1/4 cup toasted pine nuts

6 oz. feta cheese, crumbled

3 Tablespoons olive oil

Procedure

1. Place the couscous in a medium bowl.
2. Heat the broth, salt, turmeric, cumin and pepper until simmering in a small saucepan. Pour over the couscous, cover and allow the couscous to absorb all the broth, about 7 minutes.
3. Transfer the couscous to a serving bowl. Add the chopped tomatoes, cooked lentils, pine nuts, feta and olive oil and toss gently. Taste and adjust seasoning.
4. Serve warm or room temperature.

Make ahead tip: The entire recipe can be made up to 3 days ahead and served cold or room temperature.

Alternatives: The lentils can be substituted with any canned bean you like or simple omitted. You can use cooked short grain brown, steamed bulgur or wild rice in place of the couscous.

Vegetarian Dishes

I could easily be a vegetarian as I love all the foods that make up this diet. I was macrobiotic for two years in my early twenties and although it was lot of work to keep it all going, I enjoyed being that involved with what I was eating everyday. While teaching at The Natural Gourmet Cooking School in NYC for five years I found that a balanced diet is easier to achieve with the addition of animal protein. Many of my students seemed quite sickly and off kilter with all the efforts they were making to eat purely vegan. As a result I decided many years ago to include all kinds of foods in my repertoire for my benefit as well as those I cook for.

That said I still enjoy a vegetarian meal and even a couple days a week of omitting animal protein is a way to give the body a break and it helps me to feel lighter and more energized.

The variety of foods for a vegetarian is wide and interesting. Vegetables can be transformed into any number of dishes that are as satisfying and complex as meals with chicken, meat or fish. There are also quite a few recipes here that help you to learn how to cook with tofu and tempeh. Both are soy proteins that are very different in texture and flavor and lend themselves to a varied range of cooking techniques.

All the ingredients for these recipes should be organic and the freshest possible. When buying tofu be sure to pick the texture needed for the recipe, i.e. firm, soft, or silken.

I highly recommend draining your tofu and then pressing it dry on a baking sheet with a towel over it and then a plate on top. Add a weight to the plate to press out the excess water before marinating for the best flavor.

Tempeh is easy to find in health food markets and stores such as Whole Foods or Wild Oats. There a number of varieties, all worth trying so experiment with it and see which flavor you enjoy most.

I hope you come to enjoy a meat-less meal as much as I do and can have fun with creating your own delicious vegetarian dishes.

Recipes

Grilled Portobello Mushrooms with Bulgur Salad

Serves 4

Preparation time: 30 minutes

Cooking time: 10 minutes

Ingredients

1/3 cup balsamic vinegar

3/4 cup olive oil

2 cloves garlic, minced

2 Tablespoons fresh thyme, finely chopped

Salt and pepper

4 large portobello mushrooms, stems removed, wiped clean with a damp cloth

Salad:

1 1/2 cups bulgur wheat

1 3/4 cups water

1/4 cup lemon juice

1/3 cup olive oil

1/4 cup toasted pine nuts

1/2 cup chopped flat leaf parsley

1/2 cup cherry tomatoes, halved

1/4 pound parmesan cheese, shaved with a vegetable peeler, garnish

Procedure

1. Combine the vinegar, olive oil, garlic, and thyme in a shallow baking pan adding salt and pepper to taste. Scrape out the dark brown gills on the underside of the mushrooms gently with a spoon. Add to the marinade for one hour, or overnight.

2. Heat a grill pan over high heat for 5 minutes. Grill mushrooms until browned and softened turning

and basting often, about seven to 10 minutes. Reserve the leftover marinade. Transfer the mushrooms to a cutting board and allow to rest for 10 minutes.

3. Meanwhile, combine the bulgur and water in a small saucepan and bring to a boil over medium heat, cover and set aside. Allow the bulgur to sit until the water is absorbed about ten minutes. Drain off any excess water and transfer to a medium bowl, add the remaining ingredients. Season with salt and pepper to taste.

4. Divide the bulgur salad among four plates, slice the portobellos and arrange on top of the salad overlapping slightly. Drizzle the leftover marinade over the mushrooms and garnish with the shaved parmesan.

Make ahead tip: The entire recipe can be made ahead and refrigerated overnight. The mushrooms can be marinated and kept refrigerated for up to three days.

Alternatives: You can use cooked short grain brown rice in place of the bulgur and substitute tofu for the mushrooms if you prefer.

Grilled Tofu with Ginger-Sesame Marinade

Serves 4

Preparation time: 30 minutes

Marinating time: 20 minutes up to 1 week

Cooking time: 10 minutes

Ingredients

1 pound firm tofu

1/3 cup soy sauce

3 Tablespoons rice wine vinegar

2 Tablespoons toasted sesame oil

1/4 cup mirin

1 Tablespoon minced ginger

3 garlic cloves, minced

Canola oil for grilling

Peanut Sauce:

2 scallions, roughly chopped

2 garlic cloves, chopped

1 jalapeno, halved, seeded

2 1/2 Tablespoons soy sauce or tamari

2 Tablespoons lime juice

1/2 cup natural peanut butter

1/3 cup water

Noodles:

12 oz. soba noodles

1/2 red pepper, small dice, garnish

Procedure

1. Slice the tofu in half horizontally. Cover with a dish towel and place a plate on top. Weigh the tofu down with a heavy can to drain off the excess water for 20 to 30 minutes.

2. Combine the soy, rice vinegar, sesame oil, mirin, ginger and garlic in a shallow dish and add the tofu, turn to coat and marinate for at least 20 minutes.

3. Meanwhile combine all the ingredients for the peanut sauce in a food processor and puree until smooth, taste and adjust seasoning.

4. Heat a grill pan over high heat for 5 minutes. Brush the pan lightly with canola oil. Grill the tofu, reserving the marinade, for about 4 to 5 minutes on each side. Transfer to a cutting board and cut into triangles.

5. Meanwhile cook the soba noodles in a large saucepan of salted boiling water for 5 to 6 minutes, drain and transfer to a bowl. Add the reserved tofu marinade and toss well.

6. Pile the noodles onto a large serving platter top with the triangles of grilled tofu. Spoon some of the peanut sauce over the tofu and garnish with the diced red peppers. Pass the remaining peanut sauce in a small dish.

Make ahead tip: The tofu can be made ahead and kept for 1 week refrigerated in the marinade. The peanut sauce can be made ahead and kept in the freezer for up to 3 months or refrigerated for up to 7 days.

Alternatives: You can omit the peanut sauce and make more of the marinade to serve over the tofu if desired. The tofu can be served without the noodles as well.

Barley and Potato Patties with Simple Tomato Sauce

Serves 6

Preparation time: 35 minutes

Cooking time: 45 minutes

Ingredients

1 cup quick cooking barley

2 cups water

1/2 teaspoon salt

1 pound baking potatoes, peeled, cut into chunks

1 Tablespoon olive oil

1/2 onion, chopped

2 cloves garlic, minced

2 Tablespoons flat leaf parsley, chopped

1 egg

1/4 cup grated parmesan

2 oz. feta cheese, crumbled, plus more for garnish

Canola oil, for sautéing

Simple Tomato Sauce:

2 Tablespoons olive oil

1 small onion, chopped

3 garlic cloves, minced

Salt, pepper

1, 28 oz. can plum tomatoes, chopped, with their juice

1/3 cup red wine (optional)

2 teaspoons sugar or honey

10 leaves basil, chopped

Procedure

1. Combine the barley, water and salt in a medium saucepan and bring to a simmer over medium heat, cover and cook for 10 minutes. Remove from the heat and allow to sit covered for 5 minutes.

2. Place the potatoes in a saucepan of cold water, add a pinch of salt and cook until tender about 20 minutes. Drain and transfer to a large bowl. Mash with a potato masher or fork.

3. Heat a small skillet over medium high heat and add the tablespoon of olive oil. Sauté the onions and garlic for about 3 minutes. Add the sautéed onions, cooked barley, parsley, egg, and cheeses to the potatoes and combine.

4. Form the mixture into six patties. Set aside while you are making the sauce.

5. Heat the oil in a medium saucepan over medium high heat and sauté the onion and garlic for 2 minutes. Add salt, pepper, tomatoes, wine and sugar and reduce the heat to medium low. Cook, covered for 30 minutes. Add the basil and season to taste.

6. Heat a large skillet over medium high heat and add a thin layer of canola oil and sauté the patties until golden and crispy on the outside, about 4 minutes on each side.

7. Spoon some of the tomato sauce onto each plate top with the patties and garnish with crumbled feta cheese. Pass any remaining sauce at the table.

Make ahead tip: This recipe can be made ahead entirely up to 3 days ahead. The sauce can be frozen for up to 3 months. To re-heat, place the patties on a baking sheet and heat in a 350 oven for 15 minutes.

Alternatives: The barley can be substituted with cooked short grain brown rice. Feta cheese can be substituted with chevre or omitted if desired.

Tempeh Sauté with Miso Dressing

Serves 4

Preparation time: 15 minutes

Cooking time: 10 minutes

Ingredients

Dressing

3 Tablespoons canola oil

2 Tablespoons honey

2 Tablespoons miso

2 Tablespoons soy sauce or tamari

3 Tablespoons lemon juice

1 clove garlic, peeled

1 Tablespoon sesame oil

2 Tablespoons flat leaf parsley or cilantro leaves

Fresh pepper

Sauté

2 Tablespoons canola oil

1/2 red onion, halved, thinly sliced

½ pound domestic or wild mushrooms, wiped clean, thinly sliced

8 ounces Tempeh, diced

Salt and pepper, to taste

1 pound baby spinach leaves

Procedure

1. Combine the canola oil, honey, miso, tamari, lemon, garlic, sesame oil and parsley in a blender or food processor and blend until smooth, taste and add fresh pepper. Set aside.

2. Heat a large high sided skillet over medium high heat and add the canola oil. Sauté the onion until slightly golden about 5 minutes. Add the mushrooms and tempeh and continue to sauté until the tempeh is lightly browned about 8 minutes. Season well with salt and pepper. Add the spinach and quickly wilt. Add the dressing to the pan and toss gently.

3. Serve warm.

Make ahead tip: The dressing can made ahead and kept for 10 days in the refrigerator. The tempeh can be made up to adding the spinach the day before and then add the spinach before serving.

Alternatives: Firm tofu can be used in place of the tempeh, drain it as in Tofu Salad with Sesame Cilantro Dressing on page 130. Any green leafy vegetable can be used in place of the spinach such as kale, Swiss chard, bok choy or escarole.

Stuffed Acorn Squash with Parsley Walnut Pesto

Serves 4

Preparation time: 20 minutes

Cooking time: 1 hour

Ingredients

2 acorn squash, halved, seeded

3 cups flat leaf parsley, washed, stems removed

1/2 cup walnut pieces, lightly toasted

3 cloves garlic, peeled

1/3 cup grated parmesan cheese

1/3 cup extra virgin olive oil

1/2 teaspoon salt

1/4 teaspoon pepper

4 Tablespoons grated parmesan, garnish

Procedure

1. Heat the oven to 375.

2. Place the acorn squash, cut side down on a baking sheet and bake for 40 minutes until tender. Allow to cool. Reduce the oven to 350. Scoop out most of the pulp, leaving a 1/4 inch with the shell intact. Cut the halves into half again; there will be eight wedges.

3. Transfer the pulp to a food processor. Add the parsley, walnuts, garlic, cheese, and olive oil. Process until smooth. Add salt and pepper and taste for seasoning. If the mixture is too thick, add water to adjust the consistency to form a thick puree.

4. Scoop the pesto into the squash shells and bake for 10 to 15 minutes until the filling is hot. Serve warm garnished with grated parmesan.

Make ahead tip: The recipe can be made up to 3 days ahead and re-heated in a 350 oven for 15 minutes in an oblong baking dish.

Alternatives: Basil can be used in place of the parsley and pine nuts, almonds or hazelnuts can be substituted for the walnuts.

Tofu Salad with Sesame Cilantro Dressing

Serves 4

Preparation time: 40 minutes

Cooking time: 15 minutes

Ingredients

Dressing:

1/2-inch piece of peeled ginger

2 cloves garlic, peeled

1 jalapeno, seeded

4 Tablespoons soy sauce

3 Tablespoons rice vinegar

2 teaspoons brown sugar

1 Tablespoon toasted sesame oil

5 Tablespoons canola oil

4 Tablespoons cilantro leaves

3 Tablespoons mint leaves

Salad:

1 pound firm tofu

2 Tablespoons soy sauce

1 Tablespoon toasted sesame oil

1 1/2 cups shredded Napa cabbage

1 1/2 cups baby spinach leaves

1 cup shredded red cabbage

1/2 small jicama, peeled, julienne

1 medium carrot, peeled, julienne, blanched, refreshed

2 teaspoons black and white sesame seeds, toasted. garnish

Procedure

1. Combine the ginger, garlic and jalapeno in a processor and process until chopped finely. With the machine running add the soy, vinegar, sugar, canola and sesame oils. Taste and adjust seasoning. Add the cilantro and mint and process to chop the herbs. Set aside.

2. Slice the tofu in half horizontally. Cover with a dish towel and place a plate on top. Weigh the tofu down with a heavy can to drain off the excess water for 20 to 30 minutes. Then cut into 1/2-inch cubes and transfer to a baking sheet and toss with the soy sauce and sesame oil.

3. Heat the oven to 350. Meanwhile, combine the cabbage, spinach, red cabbage, jicama and carrots in a large bowl. Toss with about a half cup of the dressing.

4. Bake the tofu until browned and slightly crisp about 15 minutes

5. Divide the salad between 4 dinner plates. Top with the tofu and sesame seeds. Drizzle each with the remaining dressing and serve.

Make ahead tip: The salad and dressing can be made 3 days ahead and dressed before serving. The dressing will last up to a week in the refrigerator.

Alternatives: Tempeh can be used in place of the tofu, omit the pressing out of the water and simply marinate before baking. Mixed greens can be used in place of the cabbages and spinach. Roasted almonds, cashews or pine nuts can be substituted for the sesame seeds.

Desserts

I really love chocolate; therefore the dessert section of this book is limited to a few fruit desserts and then chocolate in various incarnations.

When buying chocolate for baking be sure to look for good quality chocolate that is something you would enjoy eating. It is best to buy chocolate that isn't referred to as baking chocolate (un-sweetened chocolate is an exception to this rule). I recommend trying different brands to discover one that suits you. With the huge surge of chocolate popularity these days there are a number of companies that are producing fabulous chocolate. It used to be widely known that the Swiss and Belgians were the master chocolate makers, but now we have chocolate made all over the world and some terrific ones here in the United States.

Baking is a science and the ingredients need to be properly measured. You can get so good at baking that you can throw things in and improvise, but until you have mastered the recipe it is best not to start with this approach if you want a dessert to enjoy.

I often make these recipes ahead and freeze them - this is especially good for cookies and some cakes.

Dessert is an important part of the meal for most of us. Some people can live on sweet things so remember to make something even if it's just sliced oranges with Grand Marnier and shaved chocolate- that recipe will be in my next book!

Recipes

Chocolate Amaretto Cake

Serves 8

Preparation time: 30 minutes

Cooking time: 45 minutes

Ingredients

10 large size Amaretti cookies, both halves, about 2 1/4 cups

4 oz. semi sweet chocolate

8 Tablespoons unsalted butter

1 cup sugar

5 large eggs, separated

1/2 cup flour

1 Tablespoon almond, orange or coffee liqueur

Confectioners' sugar, garnish

Whipped cream or ice cream, optional

Procedure

1. Heat the oven to 350. Butter a 10-inch spring form pan.

2. Grind the Amaretti and chocolate in a blender or processor until it is a fine powder. Set aside.

3. Cream the butter and sugar together in an electric mixer with the whisk attachment, and add the yolks one at a time. Beat until light colored and thickened about 4 minutes.

4. Gradually add the flour and the chocolate mixture, beating after each addition. Add the liqueur and mix. Transfer to a large mixing bowl.

5. In a clean dry bowl of an electric mixer, beat the egg whites until stiff. Lighten the amaretti mixture by stirring in a third of the egg whites. Fold in the remaining egg whites being careful not to over mix. Spoon into the prepared pan and bake for 45 minutes.

6. Allow to cool for 30 minutes and remove sides, dust with confectioners' sugar and serve with

whipped cream or ice cream if desired.

Make ahead tip: The cake can be made a week ahead and kept in the freezer or refrigerator wrapped well in plastic wrap.

Alternatives: You can use vanilla in place of the liqueur if desired.

Chocolate Biscotti

Makes 4 dozen

Preparation time: 30 minutes

Cooking time: 50 minutes

Ingredients

1 1/4 cups skinned hazelnuts, toasted and roughly chopped

1 3/4 cups flour

2/3 cup Dutch process cocoa powder

2 teaspoons baking powder

1/2 teaspoon salt

1 1/4 cups sugar

4 large eggs

1 teaspoon vanilla

Procedure

1. Heat the oven to 325. Grease two baking sheets and set aside.
2. Mix the nuts, flour, cocoa, baking powder in a large bowl. Set aside.
3. Combine the eggs, sugar and vanilla in a small bowl and beat well. Add to the dry ingredients and mix to combine.
4. Turn the dough out onto a floured cutting board and then divide in half. Roll each half into a log 14 inches long by 2 inches wide. Place the logs on the two baking sheets and flatten slightly. Bake until a toothpick comes out clean about 30 minutes. Remove from the oven and cool completely.
5. Transfer the biscotti to a cutting board. Slice in thin diagonal slices with a serrated knife and place onto the baking sheets. Bake another 20 minutes until crisp. Cool before serving.

Make ahead tip: These cookies can be made ahead and frozen for up to 3 months. You can store them in an airtight container for up to 2 weeks.

Alternatives: Other nuts can be used for biscotti such as almonds or pistachios.

Ginger Cake with Tropical Fruit Salad

Serves 8

Preparation time: 40 minutes

Cooking time: 50 minutes

Ingredients

3 large eggs

1 cup molasses

1 cup canola oil

1 cup sugar

1 teaspoon ground cloves

1 teaspoon ground cinnamon

1 teaspoon ground ginger

2 cups sifted flour

2 teaspoons baking soda

1/8 cup hot water

Fruit:

1/2 cup fresh orange juice

1/2 cup water

1/4 cup sugar

1 vanilla bean, split down the middle

5 whole cloves

1 cinnamon stick

1, 3-inch peel of orange rind

1 pineapple, diced

2 kiwis, diced

1 pint strawberries, hulled and halved

1 orange cut into small squares

Procedure

1. Heat the oven to 350. Grease a 12 x 14 baking pan.

2. Beat the eggs, molasses and oil in a large bowl until smooth.

3. Combine the sugar, spices and flour in a separate bowl. Dissolve the baking soda in the hot water in a small dish. Add the dry ingredients to the molasses mixture along with the baking soda slurry and beat well.

4. Add 1 cup of boiling water to the cake batter and beat quickly. Pour into the prepared pan and bake until a toothpick comes out clean about 45 minutes.

5. Meanwhile combine the orange juice, water, sugar, vanilla, cinnamon and orange rind in a small saucepan. Bring to a simmer and cook for 10 minutes. Allow to cool for 20 minutes or longer. Mix the pineapple, kiwis, strawberries and oranges in a medium serving bowl. Strain the syrup over the fruit and toss gently.

6. Serve the cake cut into squares with the fruit salad on the side.

Make ahead tip: The cake can be made ahead and stored in the refrigerator for up to 1 week. It can also be frozen for up to 3 months.

Alternatives: Serve the cake with applesauce or whipped cream and omit the fruit salad if desired.

Apple-Filled Crepes with Caramel Sauce

Serves 10 to 12

Preparation time: 40 minutes

Cooking time: 1 hour

Ingredients

4 large eggs

1 1/2 cups milk

1 1/2 cups all purpose flour

1/4 teaspoon salt

6 Tablespoons unsalted butter, melted and cooled slightly, plus extra for the crepe pan

Filling:

6 large granny smith apples

4 Tablespoons unsalted butter

1/3 cup sugar

2 teaspoons vanilla

1 teaspoon cinnamon

Pinch of salt

Caramel Sauce:

1 1/2 cups sugar

1/2 cup water

3 Tablespoons unsalted butter

1 cup heavy cream

Whipped cream or ice cream, if desired

Procedure

1. Combine eggs and milk in a blender and blend for 30 seconds. Add flour and salt and blend again. Transfer to a sieve over a quart size measuring cup or pitcher and strain the batter. Allow to rest for 30 minutes.

2. Add the melted and cooled butter to the batter and whisk.

3. Melt a small amount of butter in a crepe pan and add a 1/4 cup of the batter to the pan. Swirl the pan right away to cover the bottom completely. Cook about 1 minute and then flip over. Cook the until golden about 2 minutes.

4. Transfer the crepe to a baking sheet and continue until all the crepes are made.

5. Peel, core and dice the apples. Melt the 4 Tablespoons of butter in a large skillet over medium high heat and sauté the apples for 3 minutes. Add sugar and cover, reduce heat to medium-low and cook about 3 minutes. Uncover, continue to cook until softened and some of the juices have evaporated about 3 to 4 minutes, stirring occasionally. Add the vanilla, cinnamon and a pinch of salt and set aside to cool.

6. Heat the oven to 350. Butter a large gratin dish. Arrange crepes on a work surface and fill with a spoonful of apples, using a slotted spoon. Fold each crepe in half and then in half again to make a triangle. Arrange them in the dish overlapping slightly.

7. Meanwhile, in a medium saucepan combine the sugar with the water and cook, stirring over high heat until the sugar dissolves. Boil without stirring, occasionally brushing the sides down with a wet pastry brush until it begins to turn caramel colored, about 20 minutes. Remove from the heat, whisk in the butter and slowly add the cream. Return to the heat and continue to cook the caramel until it is smooth, stirring often.

8. Drizzle half of the sauce over the crepes. Bake for 15 minutes. Serve with whipped cream or ice cream if desired and pass the remaining sauce.

Make ahead tip: The crepes can made ahead and frozen for up to 3 months. The filling and caramel sauce can be made up to 3 days ahead. The entire recipe can be made up to a day ahead and reheated in a 350 oven for 20 minutes.

Alternatives: You can use pears, plums or peaches in place of the apples. Berries can also be used by omitting step 5. Toss the berries with sugar and cinnamon and fill as described above. Chocolate sauce is a good substitute for the caramel.

Makes one 9-inch tart

Preparation time: 40 minutes

Cooking time: 40 minutes

Chilling time: 30 minutes

Ingredients

Dough:

1 cup flour

Pinch salt

1 Tablespoon sugar

4 oz. unsalted cold butter, cut into bits

2 Tablespoons cold water

Filling:

1 cup blanched almonds

1/2 cup sugar

2 large eggs

Zest of one lemon

4 firm pears, peeled, cored, sliced 1/4 inch

1 cup apricot or raspberry preserves

1 Tablespoon dark rum or vanilla

Whipped cream, optional

Procedure

1. Place the flour, salt and sugar into the processor and process 30 seconds. Add butter through the feed tube one at a time. Add the water and process until the dough forms a ball. Wrap in wax paper and flatten into a disk. Chill at least thirty minutes.

2. Allow the dough to come to room temperature and roll out on a lightly floured work surface into a large round. Fit into the tart pan and press into the sides. Roll over the top with rolling pin to cut off any excess dough.

3. Heat the oven to 375.

4. Grind the almonds in a food processor, just until fine, being careful that the meal does not turn to paste. Transfer the ground almonds to a medium bowl and add the sugar, eggs, and lemon zest and mix well. Spread the filling over the bottom of the tart dough.

5. Lay the pears over the filling in concentric circles overlapping slightly.

6. Heat the preserves in a small saucepan and add the rum. Stir to dissolve preserves. Strain about half the preserves through a sieve over the tart.

7. Bake until golden and bubbly about 40 minutes. Cool on a wire rack and then remove tart sides. Transfer the tart to a serving platter and brush the remaining preserves over the top and crust. Serve with whipped cream if desired.

Make ahead tip: The tart can be made 2 days ahead and served at room temperature or slightly warm. The dough can be frozen for up to 3 months.

Alternatives: Granny smith apples can be used in place of the pears. Hazelnuts can be substituted for the almonds if desired.

Phyllo Bundles with Figs and Almonds

Serves 6

Preparation time: 30 minutes

Cooking time: 1 hour

Ingredients

1 1/4 cups dried figs

3/4 cup dry sherry, heated

3/4 cup whole almonds, ground

2 Tablespoons sugar

6 Tablespoons apricot jam

1 teaspoon ground cinnamon

24 phyllo pastry sheets , defrosted

6 Tablespoons unsalted butter, melted

Confectioners' sugar

Whipped cream, optional

Procedure

1. Place figs in a small bowl and add the warm sherry. Let stand until softened, about 30 minutes. Drain well and finely chop the figs. Mix figs, nuts, sugar, jam and cinnamon in a medium bowl.

2. Preheat the oven to 325. Spray a baking sheet with vegetable cooking spray. Stack the phyllo sheets on your work surface. Trim to a 10-inch square. Cover the stack with plastic wrap and a damp kitchen towel. Place one phyllo square on your work surface. Brush lightly with melted butter. Arrange another phyllo square on top to form a T shape. Brush lightly with butter. Repeat with two more squares, arranging corners at a slight angle.

3. Spoon 1/4 cup of the fig mixture onto the center of the phyllo stack. Lift edges of phyllo and bring together around the filling, forming a bundle. Place on the greased baking sheet. Repeat with

remaining phyllo and filling, forming a total of six bundles. Brush the outside of each bundle with melted butter.

3.   Bake until phyllo is golden about 35 minutes. Transfer the sheets to a cooling rack. Sift confectioners' sugar over the bundles and serve with whipped cream if desired.

Make ahead tip: Phyllo bundles can be made 1 day ahead. Cover carefully and chill. The filling can be made up to 5 days ahead and kept refrigerated until ready to use.

Alternatives: You can use diced apples or pears in place of the figs. Hazelnuts or pecans can be substituted for the almonds. Vanilla ice cream or frozen yogurt can be served with the bundles if desired.

Poached Pears with Red Wine Syrup

Serves 4

Preparation time: 30 minutes

Cooking time: 25 minutes

Ingredients

4 firm Bosc pears, with stems intact

1 lemon, juiced

2 strips of lemon peel, 1/2-inch wide by 2 inches long

3 cups Cabernet Sauvignon

4 Tablespoons sugar

2 cinnamon sticks

1 cup cold heavy cream

1 Tablespoon confectioners' sugar

1 teaspoon vanilla

Mint sprigs, garnish

Procedure

1. Peel the pears, halve and core them leaving 1/2 with the stem on. Drop the pears as they are peeled into a large bowl of cold water with the lemon juice.
2. In a wide high-sided saucepan combine the lemon peel, wine, sugar and cinnamon sticks. Bring to a simmer over medium heat. Simmer for 5 minutes.
3. Add the pears and lower the heat to medium-low. Cover the pan and simmer until the pears are tender when pierced with a knife about 15 minutes. Remove the pears from the wine and set aside.
4. Bring the sauce to a boil over high heat and reduce by half. Set aside and allow to cool.
5. Meanwhile whip the heavy cream in the bowl of an electric mixer with the tablespoon of

confectioners' sugar and vanilla until soft peaks form.

6. Spoon two pear halves on each dessert plate and then drizzle with some of the red wine sauce. Spoon a dollop of whipped cream on top and garnish with a mint leaf. Pass any remaining sauce.

Make ahead tip: The pears can be made up to 3 days ahead and served chilled or at room temperature.

Alternatives: Granny smith apples can be used instead. Dry white wine can be substituted for the Cabernet for a different flavor and presentation.

Bittersweet Chocolate Tart

Makes one 9-inch tart

Preparation time: 30 minutes

Cooking time: 30 minutes

Cooling time: 15 minutes

Ingredients

Dough:

1 cup flour

1/8 teaspoon salt

5 Tablespoons sugar

3 Tablespoons Dutch process cocoa powder

1/4 teaspoon baking powder

5 Tablespoons unsalted butter, cold, cut into 10 pieces

1 large egg

Filling:

3/4 cup heavy cream

1/3 cup milk

1/3 cup sugar

7 oz. bittersweet chocolate, chopped

1 large egg, beaten

1 teaspoon cocoa powder, sifted, topping

Whipped cream or ice cream, if desired

Procedure

1. Combine the flour, salt, sugar, cocoa powder and baking powder in a processor and pulse several times. Add the butter and process until mixture resembles coarse crumbs. Add the egg and pulse until dough comes together. Remove from the processor and form into a disk, wrap in wax paper

and chill for 1 hour.

2. Heat the oven to 375. Butter the bottom and sides of a 9-inch tart pan. Roll out the dough to an 11-inch circle. Fit into the pan and press into the bottom and side. Prick the bottom all over with a fork.

3. Bake about 10 to 12 minutes until well browned. Cool completely.

4. Meanwhile, in a medium saucepan combine the cream, milk and sugar and bring to a simmer over medium heat, stirring. Remove from the heat and add the chocolate. Stir until melted. Let cool to lukewarm and whisk in the egg to blend.

5. Pour the custard into the cooled shell and bake for 12 to 15 minutes until almost completely set. Transfer to a rack to cool. Sift the cocoa powder over the top of the tart and serve warm or at room temperature with the whipped cream or ice cream if desired.

Make ahead tip: The dough can be made ahead and frozen for up to 3 months. The filling can be made up to 3 days ahead. The entire tart can be made the day before serving.

Alternatives: You can use semi-sweet chocolate if you prefer a sweeter tart.

Flourless Chocolate Torte with Raspberry Coulis

Serves 10 to 12

Preparation time: 25 minutes

Cooking time: 45 minutes

Cooling time: 30 minutes

Ingredients

9 Tb. unsalted butter, room temperature

3/4 cup sugar

7 large eggs, separated

8 oz. semisweet chocolate, melted, cooled

Sauce

1 bag frozen unsweetened raspberries, defrosted

1/4 cup confectioner's sugar

2 Tb. lemon juice or raspberry liqueur

Confectioners' sugar, garnish

Whipped cream

Procedure

1. Heat the oven to 350. Grease and flour a 9-inch spring form pan.
2. Cream butter and sugar in a large bowl. Beat until fluffy and light. Add yolks, one at a time, beating until combined. Add chocolate and mix only until blended.
3. Beat the egg whites with an electric mixer until stiff peaks form.
4. Lighten the chocolate by stirring in about a third of the egg whites. Carefully fold in the remaining whites.
5. Transfer to the prepared pan and bake until a toothpick comes out clean about 40 minutes. Cool on a wire rack.

6. Meanwhile combine the berries, sugar and lemon juice in a food processor and process until smooth. Transfer to a sieve over a bowl and stir to strain out the seeds.

8. When the cake is cooled completely, remove the sides of the spring form pan. Dust with confectioners' sugar and serve with whipped cream and raspberry sauce.

Make ahead tip; You can make the cake ahead and keep it for three days in the refrigerator or freeze for up to three months. The sauce can be made ahead and stored for a week in the refrigerator or frozen.

Alternatives: Strawberries can be substituted for raspberries and ice cream can be used in place of the whipped cream.

Index

Index

Index

Index

W

Cooking is love

Amanda Cushman has been cooking for her entire adult life having begun her career in the 1980's in Manhattan.

She has traveled extensively which ignited her love of food from many cultures.

She teaches private and corporate cooking classes for groups from two to thirty and develops all her menus with an international flair.

Amanda moved to the West coast in 2003 and now makes her home in Venice California with her husband Herman and cat Sweetie.

Herman Blanke is a native of Holland and developed his passion for photography as a young adult.

He is a clean technology entrepreneur and is thrilled to live with a professional chef.

amandacooks.com